NO MOUNTAIN TOO HIGH

365 Daily Healing Thoughts

&

Prayer Journal

Patrick E. Moore

What Others Have Said, Part 1

Pat and I have been married for 48 years. We were 21 and 22 years old and straight out of college. We have definitely grown in our personal and spiritual relationships throughout the years. Our daughters, Michele and Julie, and I were blessed to have him as the spiritual leader of our home. We continue to be blessed through his daily healing messages. We are very proud of him and the publication of this book, and I know it will be a blessing to everyone who reads it. *Karen Moore, Loving Wife*

It's the first piece of information I take in every morning. Before my feet hit the floor, I read Dad's Daily Healing Thought! It's become a sweet way to begin each day. The messages are simple yet thought-provoking and always set a joyful and optimistic outlook for the day. *Michele Simpson, Daughter*

These Daily Healing Thoughts are the first thing that I do in the morning. These simple little thoughts stop me from all the chaos going around me and make me pause, take a moment and give thanks to the Lord for all the many blessings I have been given. More times than I can count, before I even read one of these, I say a quick prayer and say "Lord, let this speak to me directly." It always does. Love you, Dad. I'm so proud of you. *Julie Moore, Daughter*

Your daily healing moments are often reassuring and enlightening. At the beginning of this project, uplifting messages about healing were especially meaningful to me as I watched you manage through faith your personal healthcare condition. Most recently, I was impacted by healing words in Proverbs 2:2 about training our hearts to be good listeners and speaking hope and love to others in the country who are angry, hurting and lashing out at others in defiance. A powerful reminder and message. Thank you.

I am most thankful that you are my gifted brother. *Carole Webb Slater, Author, Sister*

When Pat told me he was going to write and publish a book about his *own healing journey,* I was not the least bit surprised! There is nothing in this earthly world that Pat is afraid to confront or take on as a challenge. You see, I have known him our entire Lives, considering we are twins and did everything together for the first 21 years. Through these years as brothers, I have witnessed everything (both good and bad) that can happen to a person. But these last two years of our lives have been very special as I have seen Pat grow as a true champion of God's Word. His thoughts, words and spiritual gifts that Pat shares in **My Daily Healing Thought,** are written by a real man (ex-Fighter Pilot, Sinner, Father, Husband and Grandfather). He is not a Preacher, Teacher or Church Deacon, but rather an *ordinary man* who has experienced an *extraordinary transformation* as a true believer in the power of God's healing. He has used historical facts, Bible quotes, and even humor, to help each person who reads this journal grow in Faith! Enjoy the journey... you will not be disappointed!"

Michael "Moose" Moore, Lt. Col, USAF(Ret), Twin Brother

Pop's healing thoughts are a great reminder each day to set aside time for God. Every time I get one of his texts, I make sure to take prayerful time to consider what his message of the day is and how I can apply it to my life. I have also greatly enjoyed getting to work with Pops on the format for his book and was the one to introduce him to the "bullet journal" concept. These healing thoughts have been an amazing bonding experience for Pops and me, and I'm so excited he's able to publish them in this book! *Jackson Peden, High School Senior and Grandson*

Pops has always been such an encourager in our family - he's always here to cheer us on during the good times and cheer us up in the bad times. His daily healing thoughts are just one of the many ways by which he shares positivity with others, and I look forward to starting each day with these uplifting messages. I love you Pops. Keep up the great work! *Mason Peden, 10th Grader and Grandson.*

Pop's daily healing thoughts are a part of my morning routine and get my mornings started. Ever since Pops started to send me the daily texts, they have become a part of me. I am very proud of Pops for devoting so much time and effort every day for the past 2 years so others can hear the Lord's words and we can now share this together every day. Pops truly is the most selfless person and such a blessing. I am so blessed he is my Grand-father. *Maddox McKim, 9th Grader and Grandson*

I've known Pat Moore for more than 25 years. He and his family are close friends of our family, and he sings in the church choir that I conduct, as well as serves in other aspects of church life. Our friendship has deepened as our faith in God has grown over the years. I admire how Pat has let God shape him into who He wants him to be. More specifically, I have been impressed with how Pat turned a difficult medical diagnosis into a vehicle to go deeper in his faith. Pat's 'take' on life and the circumstances around him have prompted some meaningful spiritual truths that he shares in this book. I hope you will be encouraged, as I have been, as you read his thoughts. *Wayne Causey, Worship Pastor*

Rarely a day goes by that I don't read Pat's "My Daily Healing Thought." Some days he makes me laugh. Some days he makes me think. Some days he makes me put my coffee mug down and pray right there. Every day he lifts up Jesus, and in so doing, lifts my eyes up to focus on Him. Thank you, Pat, for the way you connect the simple and mundane things of everyday life with the eternal truths of Jesus. Love you man! *Kevin Wood, Pat's Sunday School Teacher*

Each morning the first text message I am generally greeted by is "Daily Healing Thoughts" from my friend Pat Moore. I always look forward to this message because I know it will lift me up and that I will learn from it. Pat is a wise, godly man from whom I've much to learn. *Kent Wood, Entrepreneur*

Patrick E. Moore

For over 24 months Pat has diligently written words of hope and healing and shared his inspiration daily. Pat's tireless commitment to this effort combined with the creativity of each message has lifted the sprits of so many. Thank you, Pat, for all you have done and continue to do. *Larry Atema, President/CEO Commonwealth Development Group*

I thoroughly enjoy and look forward daily to the simple wisdom shared by Pat. Fast and easy to read, consider and apply to my daily life with Christ. *Mike Hardwick, President, CEO, Founder of Churchill Mortgage*

I look forward to Pat's Daily Healing Thoughts. I appreciate the manner in which Pat gives God credit for guiding him in his thoughts and impressions. The Healing Thoughts are practical as well as inspirational. The Bible verse references often lead to further study. Pat, thank you for answering God's calling and blessing others with your words. I am looking forward to seeing how God uses your gifts of serving Him with your unique communication skills. Blessings. *Peggy Thigpen, retired school counselor*

If you have ever spent any time with my friend Pat Moore, you would know for certain that he has the spiritual gift of encouragement. And he shares that inspiration every day through his *Daily Healing Thought*. Pat has discovered the key to improving his personal life situations by encouraging others through the scripture he observed in the ordinary. Each day, I look forward to reading what God has shown him and pray that I can find my own daily application. *John Thompson*

Healing Thoughts is a wonderful collection of daily encounters with God. Using his personal testimony supported by scripture, Pat reminds us of the many ways the Lord communicates his grace, love, peace and hope. This book will bless you! *Jacques Aebli, Regional Director, Global Media Outreach*

No Mountain Too High

I refer to one of my greatest guideposts as Uncle Pat. Anyone that looks to me for a prayer request knows about Pat. The lens of Pat's perspective delivers the light of God's word, grace and love to some dark places in my life. His prayers about gratitude, faith and miracles were spoken boldly by Pat into my life. Pat could have been a cheerleader! I never stopped praying. My prayers today are bolder and more faithful than ever. He is a true disciple. Your friend always, *Kathryn Baker Nosal*

INTRODUCTION

After my Mother died in 1985, a friend gave me a book entitled "Balcony People" written by Christian Author Joyce Landorf Heatherly, and that book changed my life forever. The book outlined two types of people in the world. Balcony people were those who stood in the balcony of your life and lifted you up, and basement people were in the basement of your life and pulled you down. My friend told me my Mother was a balcony person always lifting others up. That simple book made me think of those who had lifted me up and set me on a daily journey to be a balcony person to others.

In mid 2017, I met another Balcony Person named Erica Diggs who continually has lifted me up with her spiritual mentoring. Erica's Christian testimony included a profound passion in God's Healing Power in which I took keen interest. Less than 6months later, on January 31, 2018, I had double knee replacement and I started researching Bible verses on God's healing power. Within days of the surgery, I had a dream or vision of God touching my knees and I awoke totally at peace. I can attest I really had little pain and was amazed that four weeks later, the surgeon told me my knees were healed. I even played golf five weeks after surgery. I knew then that God's healing power was at work and I praised Him with anyone that asked me about my amazing recovery.

Then in August of 2018, I had a routine physical with that revealed an abnormal white blood count, and after follow-up tests, was given a scary diagnosis of Chronic Lymphocytic Leukemia (CLL). That was October 13, 2018. Erica started teaching me more about the gift of healing through sharing Bible verses, video sermons on healing and encouraging phone calls.

The day after the diagnosis, I committed to begin each day with prayer, Bible study and a daily journal entitled "My Daily Healing Thoughts" which has led to this book *No Mountain Too High*. For over 850 days God has inspired these inspirational thoughts, and my diagnosis has improved with no additional treatment required. By sharing these thoughts with you, I hope to lift you up.

I pray this book will be an inspiration for you regardless of whether you need healing for physical, emotional, relational or spiritual needs, because we all have issues we deal with daily.

The book is organized into daily readings so you can use it as little or as often as God leads you. There are also places to add your own prayers and notes.

Blessings

About the Book

No Mountain Too High is a compilation of my daily journal entries I began writing on October 13, 2018, after my diagnosis of chronic Lymphocytic leukemia. Originally, it was a simple spiral notebook I used to capture the daily inspiration I was receiving from books, videos and Bible verses suggested to me regarding God's Healing Power.

Next, I shifted to a more formal journal that I used for several months until my oldest grandson Jackson Peden gave me a bullet journal for my birthday in May of 2019. Jackson used this popular format for his daily calendar and journaling; he also decorated it with doodles and colors to make it fun. I asked him to teach me how to use it, and we spent about two hours coming up with the current format I use in my daily journal. In *No Mountain Too High*, I created a template to represent my daily doodles.

This book is meant to be interactive. The reader can receive my daily healing thoughts, read a key bible verse and then journal their prayers for the day. I added an entry for a blessing from the day before and express something I was thankful for each day. It has been a great help to me each day and I hope is for you.

Each day, in my journal, I draw the lines, boxes, arrows and crosses, color them, then add the daily healing thought, prayers, blessing from yesterday and thankfulness for today. I felt the time I spent each morning during the entire process was intimate time spent with my Heavenly Father. The lines were never perfect and many times my coloring was outside the lines, but those imperfections reminded me I am an imperfect man trying to move toward to perfection when I get to Heaven.

My prayer is you will participate each day with your own prayers and thankful/blessing thoughts.

Enjoy, and <u>to God be the glory!</u>

Pat

Patrick E. Moore

About the Cover

The cover of this book is an important image that goes with the theme of my Daily Healing Thoughts which is about facing all of the challenges of our life, i.e. the reference to mountains that we face.

You see, we all have mountains in our lives, whether it be an illness, fear, anxiety, marriage, fractured relationships, and more. Often, these mountains in our life seem too high to climb. The truth is we cannot scale and conquer those mountains by ourselves, but we can with JESUS and HIS WORD.

When I embarked on my own healing journey in December 2018, one of the scriptures I kept coming back to was Mark 11:23 (NIV): "Truly I tell you, if anyone says to this mountain, 'Go, throw yourself into the sea,' and does not doubt in their heart but believes that what they say will happen, it will be done for them." When I decided to write this book, I knew that the title and the image for the book cover would include mountains.

The title *NO MOUNTAIN TOO HIGH* came first and then I asked my oldest grandson Jackson Peden to design a picture that might relate to this title. He gave me this design below.

From that inspiration, our graphic designer came up with the final book cover. The image of the mountains in the distance represents the issues we face that seem too high and impossible to climb, but they are not - not with JESUS. My prayer is that *NO MOUNTAIN TOO HIGH* will help you climb and conquer those mountains.

Patrick E. Moore

Table of Contents

Patrick E. Moore

Patrick E. Moore

Patrick E. Moore

January 1

Wow, it is the 21ˢᵗ century. Sounds futuristic, huh? A New Year brings resolutions, new beginnings and the leaving of pain and struggle in the year behind us. How do we start anew? First, start with thanking GOD for the blessings HE has provided and for the blessings that are coming. Second, repeat it each day. Read **Jeremiah 29:11** and let it be your guide. "For I know the plans I have for you...". Happy New Year!

Key Bible Verse

Jeremiah 29:11 – "For I know the plans I have for you," declares the Lord, "plans to prosper you and not to harm you, plans to give you hope and a future."

Prayers & Notes

_____

_____

_____

_____

_____

_____

A Blessing from Yesterday _____

Something I am Thankful for Today _____

January 2

This morning I was reminded of a book about Jabez, a man in the Old Testament, who asked GOD to Bless him, and HE did. **1 Chronicles 4:10**. That book changed my prayer practice over 20 years ago. It also reminds me of **James 4:2,** "Ye have not because ye ask not" (KJV). Just because GOD is all knowing, doesn't mean HE doesn't expect us to ask. Ask for your Blessings today with continuing prayers of expectations. HE is waiting for us to ask.

✝

Key Bible Verse

1 Chronicles 4:10 – "Jabez cried out to the God of Israel, Oh, that you would bless me and enlarge my territory! Let your hand be with me and keep me from harm so that I will be free from pain. And God granted his request."

Prayers & Notes

_____

_____

_____

_____

_____

_____

A Blessing from Yesterday _____

Something I am Thankful for Today _____

January 3

What are the two top things most people want more of? My guess is time and money. Hopefully, we can all agree that both of those things come from our Heavenly FATHER. **Proverbs 11:24** says "one man gives freely, yet gains even more; another withholds unduly, but comes to poverty". Bottom line, want more time? Give more time to GOD. Want more money? Give more money to GOD's Kingdom. Give it a try!

Key Bible Verse

Proverbs 11:24 – "One person gives freely, yet gains even more; another withholds unduly, but comes to poverty."

Prayers & Notes

_____

_____

_____

_____

_____

_____

_____

A Blessing from Yesterday _____

Something I am Thankful for Today _____

January 4

What I learned over 13 months of recording my healing thoughts, is that healing is more than just physical. God's healing touch is about healing our body, our mind, our heart, our emotions, and our spiritual condition. **Mark 11:23** tells us to "speak to the mountain" in our life and ask GOD to remove it and cast it in the sea...in JESUS' name. Nothing is impossible. Speak to your "mountain" today!

Key Bible Verse

Mark 11:23 - "Truly I tell you, if anyone says to this mountain, 'Go, throw yourself into the sea,' and does not doubt in their heart but believes that what they say will happen, it will be done for them."

Prayers & Notes

_____

_____

_____

_____

_____

_____

A Blessing from Yesterday _____

Something I am Thankful for Today _____

Patrick E. Moore

January 5

Do you pull for the underdog? I do. My favorite Bible story of an underdog is David vs. Goliath in 1 **Samuel 17**. Newsflash: David was underestimated, and Goliath was the real underdog because he didn't have GOD on his side. Sometimes our physical or emotional struggle makes us feel like an underdog, but like David, we have GOD on our side. Read **1 Samuel 17: 36-37**. GOD will help us win. Give HIM the Glory!

Key Bible Verse

1 Samuel 17: 36-37 – "Your servant has killed both the lion and the bear; this uncircumcised Philistine will be like one of them, because he has defied the armies of the living God. The LORD who rescued me from the paw of the lion and the paw of the bear will rescue me from the hand of this Philistine."

Prayers & Notes

_____

_____

_____

_____

_____

_____

_____

A Blessing from Yesterday _____

Something I am Thankful for Today _____

January 6

Do you know people who can fix anything? I do, and I am not one of them. They just have a mechanical mind and are certainly handy to have around. It reminds me that sometimes we get mechanical about the way we worship GOD, and we lose our passion. Without passion, we cannot grow in our Faith nor be an effective witness. A Christian without passion is like a river without water. Praise HIM! **Jeremiah 20:13**.

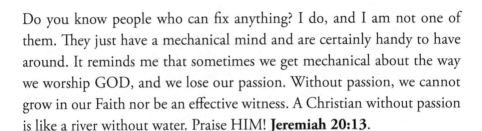

Key Bible Verse

Jeremiah 20:13 – "Sing to the LORD! Give praise to the LORD! He rescues the life of the needy from the hands of the wicked."

Prayers & Notes

_____

_____

_____

_____

_____

_____

_____

A Blessing from Yesterday _____

Something I am Thankful for Today _____

Patrick E. Moore

January 7

Blessings are precious gifts from GOD, yet too often we forget about them and hang onto our failures forever. Think of your failures as stepping-stones towards GOD's Purpose for your life. Abraham, David, Moses, Elijah and Peter all had failures that they confessed, and then GOD used them in mightier ways. Remember, your failures can't separate you from the love of GOD. **Romans 8:35-39**.

Key Bible Verse

Romans 8:38-39 – "For I am convinced that neither death nor life, neither angels nor demons, neither the present nor the future, nor any powers, neither height nor depth, nor anything else in all creation, will be able to separate us from the love of God that is in Christ Jesus our Lord."

Prayers & Notes

_____

_____

_____

_____

_____

_____

A Blessing from Yesterday _____

Something I am Thankful for Today _____

January 8

I am sure you know some people who are very wise and others who are just plain foolish. I sure do. Have you ever wondered why that is and where come from? Interesting, it has little to do with IQ? In Proverbs, it is written that the fear of the LORD is the beginning of knowledge which leads to wisdom (**Proverbs 1:7**). Today, my prayer is that we seek GOD's Wisdom in all that we say and do. Avoid being foolish!

Key Bible Verse

Proverbs 1:7 – "The fear of the LORD is the beginning of knowledge, but fools despise wisdom and instruction."

Prayers & Notes

_____

_____

_____

_____

_____

_____

A Blessing from Yesterday _____

Something I am Thankful for Today _____

Patrick E. Moore

January 9

Visualize a small child with his face bowed, eyes down and lower lip sticking out and quivering. Got it? Now think of taking that child's head in your hand and lifting it up to ask, "Child, what is wrong?" That's exactly the picture gave to us in **Psalms 3:3**. We when are struggling as a child of GOD, our Heavenly FATHER lifts our head high to comfort us. How awesome is that? Praise the one who lifts our head high! Blessings

Key Bible Verse

Psalms 3:3 – "But you, LORD, are a shield around me, my glory, the One who lifts my head high."

Prayers & Notes

_____

_____

_____

_____

_____

_____

_____

A Blessing from Yesterday _____

Something I am Thankful for Today _____

January 10

One morning, under the moonlit skies, my eyes kept focusing on the branches of the trees in our yard. Each branch different and unique from the other, like us. Trees are the most mentioned living thing in the BIBLE. Trees are mentioned in the first chapter of Genesis and the last chapter of Revelation. JESUS is the Tree of Life, and we are the branches. Remember, HE died on a tree so we wouldn't have to. **Galatians 3:13**. Praise HIM!

Key Bible Verse

Galatians 3:13 – "Christ redeemed us from the curse of the law by becoming a curse for us, for it is written: "Cursed is everyone who is hung on a pole."

Prayers & Notes

_____

_____

_____

_____

_____

_____

A Blessing from Yesterday _____

Something I am Thankful for Today _____

January 11

Have you have ever wanted to take a "mulligan" in life? You know, have you wanted a "do over" for a bad decision or choice you have made? We all have, and maybe that's the time to start over. The Bible is full of stories of people starting over, most notably Paul, who started over after an encounter with the HOLY SPIRIT on a dusty road. Remember Paul's words about starting over in **Ephesians 4:23-24**, "be renewed in the Spirit of your mind today." Praise HIM!

Key Bible Verse

Ephesians 4:23-24 – "to be made new in the attitude of your minds; and to put on the new self, created to be like God in true righteousness and holiness."

Prayers & Notes

_____

_____

_____

_____

_____

_____

_____

A Blessing from Yesterday _____

Something I am Thankful for Today _____

January 12

Ever hear the phrase "don't borrow trouble?" It's a figurative phrase that comes from the mid 1800's and means don't worry about something until it's time to worry. That phrase may have come from **Matthew 6:34** where JESUS said "therefore, do not worry about tomorrow, for tomorrow will worry about itself." Most of us worry about things that never even come to pass. We need to stop worrying!

Key Bible Verse

Matthew 6:34 – "Therefore do not worry about tomorrow, for tomorrow will worry about itself. Each day has enough trouble of its own."

Prayers & Notes

_____

_____

_____

_____

_____

_____

_____

A Blessing from Yesterday _____

Something I am Thankful for Today _____

Patrick E. Moore

January 13

Sluggard and slothful are synonyms for the word lazy, and the Bible, especially Proverbs, has a lot to say about laziness. Why? I think GOD makes it clear we cannot grow physically, financially or even spiritually if we are lazy. GOD gives us a standard to follow regarding hard work and a person, in JESUS, to emulate. Their work on our behalf never ceases. **John 5:17.** Let us put some hard work in growing our Faith today!

Key Bible Verse

John 5:17 – "In his defense Jesus said to them, 'My Father is always at his work to this very day, and I too am working.'"

Prayers & Notes

_____

_____

_____

_____

_____

_____

_____

A Blessing from Yesterday _____

Something I am Thankful for Today _____

January 14

I always marvel at how GOD uses ordinary people to do extraordinary things. The Bible story of Gideon and his 300 soldiers who saved Israel is one of those stories. **Jude 6-8**. You see, GOD can take the least of us to do great things for the Kingdom. But, before we "can do," HE calls us "to be." If we change our hearts, HE will surely use us. **1 Samuel 16:7**. It's time for us "to be" a servant of GOD so we "can do" HIS work.

✝

Key Bible Verse

1 Samuel 16:7 – "But the LORD said to Samuel, "Do not consider his appearance or his height, for I have rejected him. The LORD does not look at the things people look at. People look at the outward appearance, but the LORD looks at the heart."

Prayers & Notes

_____

_____

_____

_____

_____

_____

A Blessing from Yesterday _____

Something I am Thankful for Today _____

Patrick E. Moore

January 15

Webster's says sacrifice is the act of giving up something you want to get something else or to help someone. It reminds me of a friend who said all she wanted was peace, a peace that passes all understanding. Read **Philippians 4:7**. So what must we give up or sacrifice for that peace? We must give up anger, worry, pride, envy and anything else that separates us from our Heavenly Father. May we all seek HIS peace today!

Key Bible Verse

Philippians 4:7 – "And the peace of God, which transcends all understanding, will guard your hearts and your minds in Christ Jesus."

Prayers & Notes

_____
_____
_____
_____
_____
_____
_____
_____

A Blessing from Yesterday _____

Something I am Thankful for Today _____

January 16

When I was a boy, I can remember Pappy saying, "Any day now...," when I asked when the next calf would be born, or when the hay would be ready to cut, or when would the new Sears catalog would arrive. It was his way of saying "soon." That phrase came to me this morning as I was praying. Jesus told the disciples in **Matthew 24:36** that no one will know the hour He comes back. Are you ready for HIM? It could be any day now!

✝

Key Bible Verse

Matthew 24:42 - "Therefore keep watch, because you do not know on what day your Lord will come."

Prayers & Notes

_____

_____

_____

_____

_____

_____

_____

_____

A Blessing from Yesterday _____

Something I am Thankful for Today _____

January 17

Back in the 1700's, deerskins were traded like currency, and that is where we got the term "buck" for money. The phrase "better bang for your buck" means better value for your time or money invested. My prayer each morning is that we will be a shining light in a world of darkness. Examine your Spirit-filled efforts each day. GOD has given us more than we deserve. Is HE getting back any "bang for HIS buck?"

Key Bible Verse

Romans 5:8 – "But God demonstrates his own love for us in this: While we were still sinners, Christ died for us."

Prayers & Notes

_____

_____

_____

_____

_____

_____

_____

_____

_____

A Blessing from Yesterday _____

Something I am Thankful for Today _____

January 18

On a rainy day, I wonder where all the rain goes. Much goes underground. There is 1000 times more water under the ground than on the surface. It reminds me that as our Heavenly Father, GOD gives us HIS Living Water to live in us. His HOLY supply is more than 1000 times what we need, but we can only get it through prayer and the reading of HIS WORD. Drink of it each day and you will thirst no more. **John 4:14**

Key Bible Verse

John 4:14 – "but whoever drinks the water I give them will never thirst. Indeed, the water I give them will become in them a spring of water welling up to eternal life."

Prayers & Notes

_____

_____

_____

_____

_____

_____

A Blessing from Yesterday _____

Something I am Thankful for Today _____

Patrick E. Moore

January 19

Snowflakes are a beautiful reminder of GOD's creation. Just like us, they are each different. People didn't know they were different until 1893 when a snowflake was photographed under a microscope by a teenager named Willie Bentley. The Bible mentions snow two dozen times, mainly relating to Creation or Purity. By JESUS wiping away our sins with HIS blood, we are made white as snow. **Isaiah 1:18**. Praise HIM.

✝

Key Bible Verse

Isaiah 1:18 - "Come now, let us settle the matter, says the LORD. 'Though your sins are like scarlet they shall be as white as snow; though they are red as crimson, they shall be like wool.'"

Prayers & Notes

_____

_____

_____

_____

_____

_____

_____

A Blessing from Yesterday _____

Something I am Thankful for Today _____

January 20

I once heard a winning coach once say, "luck is where opportunity meets preparation." I don't believe in luck but in GOD's appointments. I believe GOD provides the opportunity and we must have the desire to seize the opportunity. How do we get desire? **Psalms 37:3-5** says, "if we delight in the LORD, HE will give us the desires of our heart." Praise HIM!

Key Bible Verse

Psalms 37:4 – "Take delight in the LORD, and he will give you the desires of your heart."

Prayers & Notes

_____

_____

_____

_____

_____

_____

_____

_____

_____

A Blessing from Yesterday _____

Something I am Thankful for Today _____

Patrick E. Moore

January 21

Wisdom is a gift from The HOLY SPIRIT and is the perfection of our faith through knowledge. Wisdom comes from our faith experiences when we see GOD working in our lives. Through our daily challenges, if we lean on GOD's WORD, we gain more wisdom. Then when a major life challenge occurs, we have the wisdom needed to lean on the Faith GOD has given us. Seek HIS Wisdom daily. We all need it. **James 1:5**

Key Bible Verse

James 1:5 – "If any of you lacks wisdom, you should ask God, who gives generously to all without finding fault, and it will be given to you."

Prayers & Notes

_____

_____

_____

_____

_____

_____

_____

A Blessing from Yesterday _____

Something I am Thankful for Today _____

January 22

Here is a question: in what do you really trust for your happiness? Is there something you would get angry or despondent over if you lost it? Anything other than trust in your Heavenly FATHER could or has become an idol of worship. Take inventory, and don't let your phone, work, habits, family or romantic interest replace GOD in finding happiness. We can handle any challenge if we TRUST in HIM completely. **Proverbs 3:5**.

Key Bible Verse

Proverbs 3:5 – "Trust in the LORD with all your heart and lean not on your own understanding;"

Prayers & Notes

_____

_____

_____

_____

_____

_____

_____

_____

A Blessing from Yesterday _____

Something I am Thankful for Today _____

Patrick E. Moore

January 23

The dreaded 'check engine' light usually gets my attention. How about you? I usually take quick action to find out what's wrong and get it fixed. It would be cool if GOD had given us a "check Faith" light that would flash when things go wrong in our lives physically, emotionally or spiritually. Sometimes, we could use a Spiritual checkup or a Faith tune-up. GOD's WORD can be accessed from anywhere 24/7. Check out **1 Peter 1:7**. Amen!

Key Bible Verse

1 Peter 1:7 – "These have come so that the proven genuineness of your faith—of greater worth than gold, which perishes even though refined by fire—may result in praise, glory and honor when Jesus Christ is revealed."

Prayers & Notes

_____

_____

_____

_____

_____

_____

_____

A Blessing from Yesterday _____

Something I am Thankful for Today _____

January 24

I woke up thinking about wells this morning, and I prayed for the nearly one billion people who don't have access to clean water. Then, I thought about how GOD's love for us is like an artisan well with an unlimited supply of HIS Living Water. **John 4:14** says "whoever drinks of it will have a spring of water welling up to eternal life." Drink of it now and every day, and thirst no more!

✝

Key Bible Verse

John 4:14 – "but whoever drinks the water I give them will never thirst. Indeed, the water I give them will become in them a spring of water welling up to eternal life."

Prayers & Notes

_____

_____

_____

_____

_____

_____

_____

A Blessing from Yesterday _____

Something I am Thankful for Today _____

January 25

The feeling of loneliness is not an isolated thing and sometimes becomes contagious to others. GOD doesn't want us to be lonely, and the good news is we are not alone. GOD through the HOLY SPIRIT is always with us. In **Matthew 28:20**, JESUS tells this to the disciples before HE departs for Heaven. Feeling lonely? Remember, GOD will never leave you or forsake you. **Deuteronomy 31:6**. May your Heavenly FATHER hold you close this day!

Key Bible Verse

Matthew 28:20 – "and teaching them to obey everything I have commanded you. And surely I am with you always, to the very end of the age."

Prayers & Notes

_____

_____

_____

_____

_____

_____

_____

A Blessing from Yesterday _____

Something I am Thankful for Today _____

January 26

Many people have strong opinions and voice them with confidence. I know I do. We must remember opinions are not always based on fact or knowledge, and wisdom comes with knowing when, how and to whom we share our opinions. **Proverbs 18:2** says fools are those that don't want understanding, but just want to express an opinion. Remember, our example is more important than our opinion. Live like JESUS today!

Key Bible Verse

Proverbs 18:2 – "Fools find no pleasure in understanding but delight in airing their own opinions."

Prayers & Notes

_____

_____

_____

_____

_____

_____

_____

A Blessing from Yesterday _____

Something I am Thankful for Today _____

Patrick E. Moore

January 27

Here's a critical question: what could we deny ourselves or "give up" that might bring glory to GOD? In **Luke 9:23**, JESUS told HIS Disciples "if anyone desires to follow me, let him deny himself and take up his cross daily and follow ME." The cross symbolizes death and therefore the giving up of things that are not of Christ (e.g. anger, unforgiveness, sin, etc.) means dying to ourselves. We must do this daily. What can we give up today?

✝

Key Bible Verse

Luke 9:23 – "Then he said to them all: "Whoever wants to be my disciple must deny themselves and take up their cross daily and follow me."

Prayers & Notes

_____

_____

_____

_____

_____

_____

_____

A Blessing from Yesterday _____

Something I am Thankful for Today _____

January 28

Trouble is a common word and could mean pain, sorrow, grief, brokenness, illness, loss, etc. It's common because trouble affects us all. Tribulation is a synonym for trouble. JESUS even tells us in **John 16:33** we will all have tribulation. Why? Because we live in a fallen world. Lingering in it with negative thoughts could cause it to persist or even worsen. JESUS calls us to be of good cheer and remember HE has overcome the world.

✝

Key Bible Verse

John 16:33 - "I have told you these things, so that in me you may have peace. In this world you will have trouble. But take heart! I have overcome the world."

Prayers & Notes

_____

_____

_____

_____

_____

_____

A Blessing from Yesterday _____

Something I am Thankful for Today _____

Patrick E. Moore

January 29

During my morning prayer, my eyes were drawn to the creek in my back-yard and the cold water peacefully finding its way downstream. It remind-ed me of **Isaiah 48:18** and the "peace like a river" we can have if we follow JESUS with heart, mind and soul. It doesn't mean we won't have gushing waters of trouble along the way, but if we stay obedient to HIM, peace will return. Find HIS peace today!

Key Bible Verse

Isaiah 48:18 – "If only you had paid attention to my commands, your peace would have been like a river, your well-being like the waves of the sea."

Prayers & Notes

_____

_____

_____

_____

_____

_____

_____

A Blessing from Yesterday _____

Something I am Thankful for Today _____

January 30

I enjoy driving through the hills of middle Tennessee. While driving east in the morning, the sunrise seems to be framed by the valleys and while driving west in the evening, the sunset seems to be resting on the trees at the top of the hills. The hills remind me of where my help comes from as written in **Psalms 121:1**. Let the hills always remind us help from the Lord is nearby. Praise HIS Name forever!

Key Bible Verse

Psalms 121:1 – "I lift up my eyes to the mountains – where does my help come from?"

Prayers & Notes

_____

_____

_____

_____

_____

_____

_____

A Blessing from Yesterday _____

Something I am Thankful for Today _____

January 31

Did you know that fire burns at 1200-1400 degrees Fahrenheit at a minimum? It can provide heat, or it can be destructive. It can also purify gold or silver, but it must be over 2000 degrees. Fire is also used in the Bible to describe GOD's radiance and power to purify us from our sins. Today, may the fire of GOD's light burn hot in our heart to purify our thoughts, words and deeds. Praise HIM always and don't let HIS fire go out.

Key Bible Verse

Isaiah 48:10 – "See, I have refined you, though not as silver; I have tested you in the furnace of affliction."

Prayers & Notes

_____

_____

_____

_____

_____

_____

_____

_____

A Blessing from Yesterday _____

Something I am Thankful for Today _____

February 1

Yesterday, I heard a speaker share that his wife collected rocks given to her by her grandkids from the places they visit. Even though I didn't keep my grandkids' rocks, it did get me thinking about the Rock in my life: JESUS. **Psalms 18:1-3** says the LORD is our Rock, our Fortress and our Savior. He is our Protection, our Shield, our source of power, and our place of Safety. Rest on HIM today!

✝

Key Bible Verse

Psalms 18:2 – "The Lord is my rock, my fortress and my deliverer; my God is my rock, in whom I take refuge, my shield and the horn of my salvation, my stronghold."

Prayers & Notes

_____

_____

_____

_____

_____

_____

_____

A Blessing from Yesterday _____

Something I am Thankful for Today _____

February 2

What do you do for the sheer joy of it? I am talking about pure joy with no expectations. Being with my grandkids is one thing that comes to mind and sharing my healing thoughts each morning is another. Did you know that GOD created us for HIS joy? HE created us in HIS likeness, and HE wants us to have joy. **John 15:11**. The more you can live for and with joy, even during tough times, the more you will be blessed.

✝

Key Bible Verse

John 15:11 – "I have told you this so that my joy may be in you and that your joy may be complete."

Prayers & Notes

_____

_____

_____

_____

_____

_____

_____

_____

A Blessing from Yesterday _____

Something I am Thankful for Today _____

February 3

The greatest Faith statement you can make to a non-believer is to tell them you have felt GOD's presence and know what HE has done in your life. This morning, while standing on the back porch talking to GOD, a noticeable gentle breeze began to blow. As the cool breeze swept across my face, I thanked HIM for being present. As **John 3:8** says, as Believers, we are to follow the winds of the HOLY SPIRIT to where HE leads us!

Key Bible Verse

John 3:8 – "The wind blows wherever it pleases. You hear its sound, but you cannot tell where it comes from or where it is going. So it is with everyone born of the Spirit."

Prayers & Notes

_____

_____

_____

_____

_____

_____

_____

A Blessing from Yesterday _____

Something I am Thankful for Today _____

February 4

This morning's thoughts are on the importance of running the race of life. As Christians, we run the race of life for the Glory of GOD. The finish line is Heaven. In **2 Timothy 4:7**, before Paul dies, he writes an encouraging letter to Timothy. It says, "I have fought the good fight and finished the race." That verse should encourage us as well, would you agree? The question is are you in the right race? Then keep fighting! Keep running!

Key Bible Verse

2 Timothy 4:7 – "I have fought the good fight, I have finished the race, I have kept the faith."

Prayers & Notes

_____

_____

_____

_____

_____

_____

_____

_____

A Blessing from Yesterday _____

Something I am Thankful for Today _____

February 5

We all know or have known someone who embodied the phrase "it's my way, or the highway." That authoritative style, in my opinion, is about pride, ego, insecurity and a controlling nature. These definitely are not a GOD-like qualities. JESUS, on the other hand, tells us "I am the way" but gives us the free will to accept that or not. **John 14:6**. This morning, let us pray to live GOD's way, not our way.

Key Bible Verse

John 14:6 – "Jesus answered, 'I am the way and the truth and the life. No one comes to the Father except through me.'"

Prayers & Notes

_____

_____

_____

_____

_____

_____

_____

A Blessing from Yesterday _____

Something I am Thankful for Today _____

Patrick E. Moore

February 6

Have you ever heard a song with lyrics that sort of take your breath away? That happened to me last night while listening to the Christian song, "I Thought by Now," by Heather Sorenson. We all have had times in our lives when our fear, doubt, pain or sin made us think that surely by now GOD has left us, abandoned us, or run out of Mercy on us. Good News! He will never leave us or forsake us! **Deuteronomy 31:6**.

Key Bible Verse

Deuteronomy 31:6 – "Be strong and courageous. Do not be afraid or terrified because of them, for the Lord your God goes with you; he will never leave you nor forsake you."

Prayers & Notes

_____

_____

_____

_____

_____

_____

_____

A Blessing from Yesterday _____

Something I am Thankful for Today _____

February 7

The snow falling this morning is peaceful, pure, and tranquil, and it makes me think of what Heaven might be like. Snow forms when dust particles collide with falling water and freeze into ice crystals. It is white because the ice crystals in the snowflake reflect light. What a great metaphor for us. GOD takes the sinful self, mixes it with HIS Living Water, and transforms us to reflect HIS LIGHT. We can become as white as snow. **Isaiah 1:18**. Praise HIM!

✝

Key Bible Verse

Isaiah 1:18 - "Come now, let us settle the matter," says the LORD. 'Though your sins are like scarlet, they shall be as white as snow; though they are red as crimson, they shall be like wool.'"

Prayers & Notes

_____

_____

_____

_____

_____

_____

_____

A Blessing from Yesterday _____

Something I am Thankful for Today _____

February 8

Real fear is natural. Take the fight or flight response as an example. The more prominent fear, however, is psychological such as the fear of failure or rejection. It's driven by ego, encouraged by Satan, and harms us physically and spiritually. Then there is the fear of the LORD, which is based on our deep love and devotion for HIM. Our fear or awe of the LORD guides us to live our lives to please and not to disappoint HIM. HE will Bless that fear. **Luke 1:50**. Seek HIM!

Key Bible Verse

Luke 1:50 – "His mercy extends to those who fear him, from generation to generation."

Prayers & Notes

_____

_____

_____

_____

_____

_____

_____

A Blessing from Yesterday _____

Something I am Thankful for Today _____

February 9

Feed companies during the 30's put their grain in colorful cotton bags that could be repurposed into clothes. Much of that spare cloth probably ended up in beautiful quilts, like the one I am sitting on, handed down from family members. Our lives are like a quilt GOD makes from patches of experiences whether sad or happy. They are stitched together by GOD's handiwork to make something beautiful and cherished. **Ecclesiastes 3:11**. Trust HIM!

✝

Key Bible Verse

Ecclesiastes 3:11 – "He has made everything beautiful in its time. He has also set eternity in the human heart; yet no one can fathom what God has done from beginning to end."

Prayers & Notes

_____

_____

_____

_____

_____

_____

_____

A Blessing from Yesterday _____

Something I am Thankful for Today _____

Patrick E. Moore

February 10

During all of the rain we've had recently, my windshield wipers have been my car's MVP. They keep the windshield clear so I can find my way safely. Our conscience is like the windshield to our Heart and Soul. Sometimes we face nasty sins and guilt, and we need to clear our consciences to find our way forward. The reading of GOD's WORD, prayer and confession of sin help clear our consciences before man and GOD. **Acts 24:16**.

Key Bible Verse

Acts 24:16 – "So I strive always to keep my conscience clear before God and man."

Prayers & Notes

_____

_____

_____

_____

_____

_____

_____

_____

A Blessing from Yesterday _____

Something I am Thankful for Today _____

February 11

Ever bought unfinished furniture? We have. I can remember buying four stools that we sanded and finished for our kitchen. They worked out great. This morning I was reminded that GOD sees us as unfinished business, because HE is not done with us yet. We all could use some good, Spiritual polishing. Stay strong and stay in HIS WORD, because HE's not finished with us. **Philippians 1:6.**

✝

Key Bible Verse

Philippians 1:6 – "being confident of this, that he who began a good work in you will carry it on to completion until the day of Christ Jesus."

Prayers & Notes

_____

_____

_____

_____

_____

_____

_____

_____

_____

A Blessing from Yesterday _____

Something I am Thankful for Today _____

February 12

There is an awesome story in **Mark 2:1-5** about friends with strong faith who went to great lengths to get their sick friend close to Jesus, because they knew JESUS could heal him. We all have friends or family who need the healing touch OF JESUS today. Even though prayer is important, maybe it's time to do something extraordinary to make sure they get closer to JESUS. Let your Faith be contagious to those in need today.

✝

Key Bible Verse

Mark 2:5 - "When Jesus saw their faith, he said to the paralyzed man, 'Son, your sins are forgiven.'"

Prayers & Notes

_____

_____

_____

_____

_____

_____

_____

_____

A Blessing from Yesterday _____

Something I am Thankful for Today _____

February 13

In ancient days, a fortress built around a city allowed the people inside to live a thriving life without worry of being attacked by enemies. As Christians, our fortress is GOD, our Heavenly Father, who is our protector and shield from present danger. Want to be a witness to your family and friends? Show them GOD is your fortress, and He gives you peace and hope even in the chaos and evil around us. Praise HIM forever!

Key Bible Verse

Psalm 18:2 - "The Lord is my rock and my fortress and my deliverer, My God, my rock, in whom I take refuge; My shield and the horn of my salvation, my stronghold."

Prayers & Notes

_____

_____

_____

_____

_____

_____

A Blessing from Yesterday _____

Something I am Thankful for Today _____

February 14

The cold temperatures this morning made me think of the old saying, "cold hands warm heart." Outward coldness does not mean you don't have a warm heart, of course. That's a myth, but the reality is sometimes the world can be cold and cruel. When the cold becomes overwhelming, cozy up in GOD's WORD and the warmth of His Spirit. In **1 Peter 1:22,** you will find that we are called to love each other with a warm heart.

✝

Key Bible Verse

1 Peter 1:22 – "Now that you have purified yourselves by obeying the truth so that you have sincere love for each other, love one another deeply, from the heart."

Prayers & Notes

_____

_____

_____

_____

_____

_____

_____

A Blessing from Yesterday _____

Something I am Thankful for Today _____

February 15

Last night was our Sunday school class' turn to host nine homeless men at our church and provide them a hot meal and warm bed on a freezing night. Sitting at the table with them made me think of when Jesus invited the outcast and downtrodden to HIS table. JESUS invites all of us to come to HIS table. Read HIS parable of whom to invite in **Luke 14**. There's always room for more. Bless HIS name forever!

Key Bible Verse

Luke 14:13-14 – "But when you give a banquet, invite the poor, the crippled, the lame, the blind, and you will be blessed. Although they cannot repay you, you will be repaid at the resurrection of the righteous."

Prayers & Notes

_____

_____

_____

_____

_____

_____

A Blessing from Yesterday _____

Something I am Thankful for Today _____

Patrick E. Moore

February 16

A tall cedar tree caught my gaze this morning. Its green leaves show it is growing even in winter. It has a strong root system that can grow in rocky soil. Its sturdy timber was used to build David and Solomon's temple. What a great analogy for GOD's people - that we become strong, with roots growing deep in GOD's Love, growing through any season, with our fruit building GOD's Kingdom. **Ephesians 3:17**. Bless HIM!

Key Bible Verse

Ephesians 3:17 – "so that Christ may dwell in your hearts through faith. And I pray that you, being rooted and established in love,"

Prayers & Notes

_____

_____

_____

_____

_____

_____

_____

_____

A Blessing from Yesterday _____

Something I am Thankful for Today _____

February 17

The evidence is clear that our emotional and mental state affects our immune system and our health. Even Harvard has many published articles on the subject. As humans, we have emotions of sadness and grief, but how we deal with them could affect if we get sick and/or how we recover. **Proverbs 17:22** tells us a merry heart is like medicine. Let GOD's WORD be your medicine today. It's free.

✝

Key Bible Verse

Proverbs 17:22 – "A cheerful heart is a good medicine, but a crushed spirit dries up the bones."

Prayers & Notes

_____

_____

_____

_____

_____

_____

_____

_____

A Blessing from Yesterday _____

Something I am Thankful for Today _____

Patrick E. Moore

February 18

There is no doubt in my mind that GOD has given us gifts that, when used according to God's will, can bring Glory to HIM. See **1 Corinthians 12:9**. And since we are all wounded in some way, HE uses us in our brokenness to share our gifts. We must study HIS WORD, Pray, have Faith, and start giving our gifts away. What we give will come back to us in greater measure. **Luke 6:38**. Thank you, FATHER, for our gifts. Help us to not waste them.

✝

Key Bible Verse

1 Corinthians 12:9 – "to another faith by the same Spirit, to another gifts of healing by that one Spirit,"

Prayers & Notes

_____

_____

_____

_____

_____

_____

_____

A Blessing from Yesterday _____

Something I am Thankful for Today _____

February 19

What does it mean to commit to something? It is your promise and willingness to dedicate yourself to something or someone. "Commit" is an action verb that requires mental and physical effort. GOD made a commitment to us by sending us HIS Son to die on the cross for us. Therefore, HE is worthy of our Praise. Commit everything you do today to GOD, and HE will establish your plans. **Proverbs 16:3**.

✝

Key Bible Verse

Proverbs 16:3 – "Commit to the LORD whatever you do, and he will establish your plans."

Prayers & Notes

_____

_____

_____

_____

_____

_____

_____

_____

A Blessing from Yesterday _____

Something I am Thankful for Today _____

Patrick E. Moore

February 20

This morning, there is heavy fog which always looks mysterious to me. It's formed when cooler air passes over warm air and limits what we can see. For me, there are many mysteries about GOD, Heaven, sickness, life and death that we cannot fully see or understand. **Corinthians 13:12** says it is like looking through a fog, but that when that day comes, we will fully see GOD as HE sees us. Praise HIS Name forever!

Key Bible Verse

Corinthians 13:12 – "For now we see only a reflection as in a mirror; then we shall see face to face. Now I know in part; then I shall know fully, even as I am fully known."

Prayers & Notes

_____

_____

_____

_____

_____

_____

_____

A Blessing from Yesterday _____

Something I am Thankful for Today _____

February 21

This morning, as I was going outside in the cool air for my prayer time, I looked down at the word "Welcome" written on the doormat. GOD reminded me that, as Christians, we are to be welcoming to everyone. We are to welcome those we can serve and also those who come to serve us when we are in time of need. My prayer today is that we all have a welcoming spirit that will be pleasing to our Heavenly Father. **Matthew 10:42**.

✝

Key Bible Verse

Matthew 10:42 – "And if anyone gives even a cup of cold water to one of these little ones who is my disciple, truly I tell you, that person will certainly not lose their reward."

Prayers & Notes

_____

_____

_____

_____

_____

_____

_____

A Blessing from Yesterday _____

Something I am Thankful for Today _____

February 22

Trust is a strong belief in something or someone. It is based on truth, ability and reliability. If I wanted a good meal, I would have more trust in a chef who wrote a cookbook than someone who is pretending and bought a chef's hat. It would be just as ridiculous for us in our effort to have a healthy, prosperous and full life, to trust in our limited wisdom and ignore the Author of creation. Trust in HIM today! **Proverbs 3:5-6**.

Key Bible Verse

Proverbs 3:5-6 – "Trust in the LORD with all your heart and lean not on your own understanding; in all your ways submit to him, and he will make your paths straight."

Prayers & Notes

_____

_____

_____

_____

_____

_____

_____

A Blessing from Yesterday _____

Something I am Thankful for Today _____

February 23

It's true that what's in your heart will be what people see on your face. If you have joy in your heart, people will see a smile on your face. **Proverbs 15:13**. Pain and sorrow reflect the opposite. How do we get joy in our hearts? I think it starts with the discipline of giving thanks each day. I pray every morning for GOD to let me shine HIS light to someone during the day, and lo and behold, HE gives me a lot to smile about. Try it!

✝

Key Bible Verse

Proverbs 15:13 – "A happy heart makes the face cheerful, but heartache crushes the spirit."

Prayers & Notes

_____

_____

_____

_____

_____

_____

_____

A Blessing from Yesterday _____

Something I am Thankful for Today _____

February 24

The idiom "the proof is in the pudding" is applicable to us in so many ways, even in our faith. You see, telling people about JESUS, the man, or that you are a Christian, is not as important as telling and showing others what HE has done in your life. In **Mark 5:19,** that is what JESUS told the possessed man after HE had removed the demons from him. Remember, the proof is in the pudding. Share what HE has done, because that can't be disputed! Praise HIM!

✝

Key Bible Verse

Mark 5:19 – "Jesus did not let him, but said, 'Go home to your own people and tell them how much the Lord has done for you, and how he has had mercy on you.'"

Prayers & Notes

_____

_____

_____

_____

_____

_____

A Blessing from Yesterday _____

Something I am Thankful for Today _____

February 25

I have always had a fascination with waterfalls. Their beauty and sound are so peaceful and comforting, but why don't they run out of water? Because of the sun. That's right, the sun shining causes water to evaporate from the oceans which causes rain to keep the rivers flowing. GOD's creation is awesome, isn't it? Let the waterfalls remind us of GOD's Love for us will always flow in our hearts. **Nehemiah 8:10.**

Key Bible Verse

Nehemiah 8:10 – "Nehemiah said, 'Go and enjoy choice food and sweet drinks, and send some to those who have nothing prepared. This day is holy to our Lord. Do not grieve, for the joy of the LORD is your strength.'"

Prayers & Notes

_____

_____

_____

_____

_____

_____

_____

A Blessing from Yesterday _____

Something I am Thankful for Today _____

Patrick E. Moore

February 26

Ever heard the expression "cry uncle?" It's an old phrase which means to submit or give up. My parents gave me competitive genes, so I don't give up easily, but we all have had people in our lives who get frustrated with us and give up on us. Fortunately, we have someone who will never give up on us, and that is our Heavenly Father. Take comfort in that today. **Joshua 1:9**

Key Bible Verse

Joshua 1:9 – "Have I not commanded you? Be strong and courageous. Do not be afraid; do not be discouraged, for the LORD your God will be with you wherever you go."

Prayers & Notes

_____

_____

_____

_____

_____

_____

_____

A Blessing from Yesterday _____

Something I am Thankful for Today _____

February 27

This morning, the dancing flame in the gas lantern lit my path down the front sidewalk, and it reminded me of the eternal light of Christ that is always shining on us. **John 1:9**. Sometimes in our human weakness and with Satan's encouragement, we wander in the shadows and away from HIS Light. Seek HIM daily with prayer and the reading of HIS WORD, so you can stay in HIS Guiding light.

Key Bible Verse

John 1:9 – "The true light that gives light to everyone was coming into the world. "

Prayers & Notes

_____

_____

_____

_____

_____

_____

_____

_____

A Blessing from Yesterday _____

Something I am Thankful for Today _____

Patrick E. Moore

February 28

As the sun comes up on the back porch of our hotel room in Scottsdale, Arizona, the mountain of rock formations is just coming into focus. Wow, what made these formations? How did the rocks get there? Did GOD place each rock in place? The southwest landscape is quite breathtaking. Interesting, rocks are mentioned over 140 times in the Bible. Remember, GOD is the rock of our salvation **Psalms 89:22**. Trust in HIM!

Key Bible Verse

Psalms 89:22 – "The enemy will not get the better of him; the wicked will not oppress him."

Prayers & Notes

_____

_____

_____

_____

_____

_____

_____

A Blessing from Yesterday _____

Something I am Thankful for Today _____

February 29

Sometimes, it's difficult to love people because of what they say or what they do. In fact, sometimes, in our sinfulness, it's hard to love ourselves. But here is the good news: JESUS doesn't love us because of the way we are, but because of who we are. We are all HIS Children, and we are made in His image (**Genesis 1:27**) to love everyone, including our enemies. We need to seek HIS WORD daily, so we don't forget it.

Key Bible Verse

Genesis 1:27 – "So God created mankind in his own image, in the image of God he created them; male and female he created them."

Prayers & Notes

_____

_____

_____

_____

_____

_____

_____

A Blessing from Yesterday _____

Something I am Thankful for Today _____

Patrick E. Moore

March 1

What do we stand for? A pastor asked that question to our group as he discussed the false religion of secularism we face today. He used the book of Daniel as a parallel to today. Shadrach, Meshach, Abednego and Daniel stood up for their faith and didn't back down. Today, as Christians, we find ourselves in a foreign land of secularism. We must take a stand. Remember the lyrics of Tom Petty's song, and don't back down.

✝

Key Bible Verse

Ephesians 6:13 – "Therefore put on the full armor of God, so that when the day of evil comes, you may be able to stand your ground, and after you have done everything, to stand."

Prayers & Notes

_____

_____

_____

_____

_____

_____

_____

A Blessing from Yesterday _____

Something I am Thankful for Today _____

March 2

The older I get, the more I realize that GOD has directed, is directing and will direct our steps in life. You see, the providence of time, people and circumstances are not accidental. There is a great example of this in Acts **8:26-40**. We see how GOD directs the steps of the Evangelist Philip and the conversion of the Ethiopian official. An entire nation began to hear about JESUS as a result. Where is GOD directing your steps? **Proverbs 16:9**. Praise HIM today!

✝

Key Bible Verse

Proverbs 16:9 – "In their hearts humans plan their course, but the LORD establishes their steps."

Prayers & Notes

_____

_____

_____

_____

_____

_____

_____

A Blessing from Yesterday _____

Something I am Thankful for Today _____

March 3

This morning I awoke to the news of loss of life and property in our city due to tornadoes. My first thought was to pray for families affected and the second was to thank GOD for keeping our family safe. There are hurting people this morning who may be asking "LORD why me?" **Philippians 3:13-14** gives us comfort that during the struggles and pain of circumstances, we need to keep our Eyes on JESUS and the eternity that follows.

Key Bible Verse

Philippians 3:13-14 – "Brothers and sisters, I do not consider myself yet to have taken hold of it. But one thing I do: Forgetting what is behind and straining toward what is ahead, I press on toward the goal to win the prize for which God has called me heavenward in Christ Jesus."

Prayers & Notes

_____

_____

_____

_____

_____

_____

A Blessing from Yesterday _____

Something I am Thankful for Today _____

March 4

Blindness would be a difficult physical challenge, and yet GOD has blessed many people who have visual impairments, including Helen Keller, Louis Braille, Ray Charles, Andrea Bocelli and many others. Spiritual blindness would be worse. There is only one that can open the eyes of the spiritually blind and it is JESUS. GOD's WORD will help you fight the darkness of Evil. Keep the eyes of your heart focused on GOD. **Isaiah 35:5**

✝

Key Bible Verse

Isaiah 35:5 – "Then will the eyes of the blind be opened and the ears of the deaf unstopped."

Prayers & Notes

_____

_____

_____

_____

_____

_____

_____

A Blessing from Yesterday _____

Something I am Thankful for Today _____

March 5

When I was young, I loved Lincoln Logs which celebrate their 100th anniversary this year. The inventor was John Lloyd Wright, the son of the famous architect. The interlocking design came from his Dad's design created for the foundation of some of his buildings to withstand earthquakes. GOD's WORD provides the foundation of our Faith, and without that foundation, our faith would crumble in the storms of life. **Matthew 7:24-25**

✝

Key Bible Verse

Matthew 7:24-25 - "Therefore everyone who hears these words of mine and puts them into practice is like a wise man who built his house on the rock. The rain came down, the streams rose, and the winds blew and beat against that house; yet it did not fall, because it had its foundation on the rock."

Prayers & Notes

_____

_____

_____

_____

_____

_____

A Blessing from Yesterday _____

Something I am Thankful for Today _____

We have had so much rain that when I walk in the grass, the ground is squishy. It's like walking on damp marshmallows. It reminded me that sometimes, even as Christians, our faith walk becomes squishy - soft, yielding, lenient and not firm. GOD's WORD and HIS character are not squishy. They are HOLY, righteous, firm and unyielding. We are to be HIS warriors and not ashamed of HIS WORD. **Romans 1:16.**

Key Bible Verse

Romans 1:16 – "For I am not ashamed of the gospel, because it is the power of God that brings salvation to everyone who believes: first to the Jew, then to the Gentile."

Prayers & Notes

_____

_____

_____

_____

_____

_____

_____

A Blessing from Yesterday _____

Something I am Thankful for Today _____

March 7

Last night, I had the blessing of hearing Heather Sorensen sing her song, "Let me walk you home," and it spoke to my heart. As a Christian, I know our home is Heaven, but sometimes that journey is difficult and scary, either for us or someone we love. Don't be afraid. Know we will have the HOLY SPIRIT to walk us Home and strengthen us to hold someone else's hand as they journey Home. Praise HIM. **Romans 15:13**

✝

Key Bible Verse

Romans 15:13 – "May the God of hope fill you with all joy and peace as you trust in him, so that you may overflow with hope by the power of the Holy Spirit."

Prayers & Notes

_____

_____

_____

_____

_____

_____

_____

A Blessing from Yesterday _____

Something I am Thankful for Today _____

March 8

Have you ever said or heard someone say, "they got what they deserved?" Of course you have, and most of the time it is true for us, too. But for Christians, there is a major exception to that rule, because GOD gave us HIS Mercy when we deserved HIS wrath. **Ephesians 2:3-5**. Maybe the next time we start to condemn someone with our wrath, we can remember this verse. Thank HIM today for HIS Grace!

Key Bible Verse

Ephesians 2:3-5 – "All of us also lived among them at one time, gratifying the cravings of our flesh and following its desires and thoughts. Like the rest, we were by nature deserving of wrath. But because of his great love for us, God, who is rich in mercy, made us alive with Christ even when we were dead in transgressions—it is by grace you have been saved."

Prayers & Notes

_____

_____

_____

_____

_____

_____

A Blessing from Yesterday _____

Something I am Thankful for Today _____

Patrick E. Moore

March 9

I took our dog on a long walk in a park yesterday. A few times, she stubbornly pulled against her leash because she wanted to go down the wrong path. Similarly, as GOD guides us, we sometimes pull back and want to go a different direction. We are not on a leash, but GOD's hands are on our shoulders, leading us. Don't resist; HE knows the way. **John 16:13**

Key Bible Verse

John 16:13 – "But when he, the Spirit of truth, comes, he will guide you into all the truth. He will not speak on his own; he will speak only what he hears, and he will tell you what is yet to come."

Prayers & Notes

_____

_____

_____

_____

_____

_____

_____

A Blessing from Yesterday _____

Something I am Thankful for Today _____

March 10

As a boy, I saw boys selling newspapers on the street shouting, "Extra! Extra! Read all about it!" especially when there was big news. Too many people I know are waiting for some big earthly news in their lives that will make them happy. Phooey. Earthly desires won't do it. The best news we can ever hear is that GOD sent HIS only begotten SON to die for our sins and give us eternal life. Extra! Extra! Read all about it in His word. **John 3:16**

✝

Key Bible Verse

John 3:16 – "For God so loved the world that he gave his one and only Son, that whoever believes in him shall not perish but have eternal life."

Prayers & Notes

_____

_____

_____

_____

_____

_____

_____

A Blessing from Yesterday _____

Something I am Thankful for Today _____

March 11

Two words came to my mind this morning: believe and healing. One means to trust without proof, and the other means to cure or make whole. In my life, they are divinely connected because I believe, GOD has healed and is healing me. "Believe" is not a magic word like "Shazam." It is a continuing mindset that is grounded in daily prayer and reading of GOD's WORD. Be patient and steadfast, and trust in GOD's timing. **Luke 8:50**

Key Bible Verse

Luke 8:50 – "Hearing this, Jesus said to Jairus, 'Don't be afraid; just believe, and she will be healed.'"

Prayers & Notes

_____

_____

_____

_____

_____

_____

_____

_____

A Blessing from Yesterday _____

Something I am Thankful for Today _____

March 12

When there are storms, virus threats, and financial downturns, many become afraid and start to think GOD's blessings have been taken away. Not true. GOD's blessings will continue for those who are faithful, especially those who endure trials. **James 1:12.** Therefore, let us lift each other up during trials and continue to be faithful to the ONE who gives us life and every perfect thing. HIS Blessings will endure forever! Amen.

✝

Key Bible Verse

James 1:12. – "Blessed is the one who perseveres under trial because, having stood the test, that person will receive the crown of life that the Lord has promised to those who love him."

Prayers & Notes

_____

_____

_____

_____

_____

_____

A Blessing from Yesterday _____

Something I am Thankful for Today _____

March 13

Wow, the mass hysteria regarding the Covid-19 virus is overblown, in my opinion, but we have no choice but deal with it. As Christians, we should know better than to let fear and anxiety affect our daily lives. I am reminded that JESUS asked the people in **Matthew 8:26** "why are ye so afraid, ye of little faith?" Pray for a revival and renewal of the HOLY SPIRIT in your family during this time. Remember, this too shall pass!

Key Bible Verse

Matthew 8:26 – "He replied, 'You of little faith, why are you so afraid?" Then he got up and rebuked the winds and the waves, and it was completely calm.'"

Prayers & Notes

_____

_____

_____

_____

_____

_____

_____

A Blessing from Yesterday _____

Something I am Thankful for Today _____

March 14

An Ulu knife was invented by Eskimos in 2500 BC. Originally made from stone with an antler handle, it was great for hunting and enabled the Eskimo to cut deep and quick through muscle and bone to harvest the meat. GOD's WORD is sharper than that. **Hebrews 4:12**, says it is sharper than a double-edged sword. It can cut deep to our soul to help us distinguish between the truth and lies. We need to seek it today more than ever!

Key Bible Verse

Hebrews 4:12 – "For the word of God is alive and active. Sharper than any double-edged sword, it penetrates even to dividing soul and spirit, joints and marrow; it judges the thoughts and attitudes of the heart. "

Prayers & Notes

_____

_____

_____

_____

_____

_____

_____

A Blessing from Yesterday _____

Something I am Thankful for Today _____

March 15

Most of us go through times in our lives where we reassess our faith. I know I sure have. They could come from a joyous mountain top experience, a struggle in the valley, or maybe just a time of uncertainty like today. A time of reflection is always good if you make sure GOD is with you. A good premise to start with is **James 1:17**, because it reminds us that everything that is good comes from GOD. Maybe it's time to hit the reset button!

Key Bible Verse

James 1:17 – "Every good and perfect gift is from above, coming down from the Father of the heavenly lights, who does not change like shifting shadows."

Prayers & Notes

_____

_____

_____

_____

_____

_____

_____

A Blessing from Yesterday _____

Something I am Thankful for Today _____

March 16

Remember fire drills in school? They began in the late 1950's after a tragic school fire in Chicago. It prompted safety guidelines and mandated fire drill practices for all schools. Think of your daily prayer and quiet time as a "spiritual fire drill" against the disasters and struggles of life. Some might say the Corona virus is a fire. Are you equipped for the struggle? Seek HIS WORD today! **Isaiah 43:2-3**

Key Bible Verse

Isaiah 43:2-3 – "When you pass through the waters, I will be with you; and when you pass through the rivers, they will not sweep over you. When you walk through the fire, you will not be burned the flames will not set you ablaze. For I am the LORD your God, the Holy One of Israel, your Savior; I give Egypt for your ransom, Cush and Seba in your stead."

Prayers & Notes

_____

_____

_____

_____

_____

A Blessing from Yesterday _____

Something I am Thankful for Today _____

Patrick E. Moore

March 17

Have you ever bought something that required instructions to install or assemble but all you found were a few pictures? Thank goodness for YouTube tutorials. You know, humans came with a really good instruction manual, and it's called the Bible. Want to know how to deal with difficult people? Look to **Luke 6:27-31,** and you will find the golden rule. Thank HIM.

Key Bible Verse

Luke 6:27-31 – "But to you who are listening I say: Love your enemies, do good to those who hate you, bless those who curse you, pray for those who mistreat you. If someone slaps you on one cheek, turn to them the other also. If someone takes your coat, do not withhold your shirt from them. Give to everyone who asks you, and if anyone takes what belongs to you, do not demand it back. Do to others as you would have them do to you."

Prayers & Notes

_____

_____

_____

_____

_____

_____

A Blessing from Yesterday _____

Something I am Thankful for Today _____

March 18

We have been using a laser level while building my garage office to make sure walls and floors are level and straight. Lasers are complex, but the result is a highly focused light beam. I am reminded that during times of uncertainty, we need our hearts and eyes to be laser focused on JESUS. Don't be distracted by Satan's fears, but stay focused on your Heavenly FATHER. **Colossians 3:1**

✝

Key Bible Verse

Colossians 3:1 – "Since then, you have been raised with Christ, set your hearts on things above, where Christ is, seated at the right hand of God."

Prayers & Notes

_____

_____

_____

_____

_____

_____

_____

_____

A Blessing from Yesterday _____

Something I am Thankful for Today _____

Patrick E. Moore

March 19

Yaks are beasts of burden located on the highlands of Asia. Their hair is similar to cashmere, and they can carry up to 800 pounds for short distances. Speaking of burdens, we all are facing them now because of the virus scare but remember they will be temporary. The Bible speaks of burdens in **2 Corinthians 4:7**. Remember, God won't let the burden get too heavy, and it will be temporary. Trust HIM!

Key Bible Verse

2 Corinthians 4:7 – "But we have this treasure in jars of clay to show that this all-surpassing power is from God and not from us."

Prayers & Notes

_____

_____

_____

_____

_____

_____

_____

A Blessing from Yesterday _____

Something I am Thankful for Today _____

March 20

Good morning! GOD is good, amen? Yes, we all have uncertainty about our family, our jobs, our country and our world, but Jehovah Jirah (one that provides) is still our GOD. This morning, GOD reminded me that HE has been there for HIS people through every disaster. Don't panic, GOD has allowed for us to have extra time, so let's use it wisely. **Isaiah 41:10.**

✝

Key Bible Verse

Isaiah 41:10 – "So do not fear, for I am with you; do not be dismayed, for I am your God. I will strengthen you and help you; I will uphold you with my righteous right hand."

Prayers & Notes

_____

_____

_____

_____

_____

_____

_____

A Blessing from Yesterday _____

Something I am Thankful for Today _____

March 21

Most interstates in the country use rumble strips on the shoulders to alert drivers and help reduce accidents due to drowsiness or distractions. Maybe we need some divine rumble strips as we travel life's highway to keep our minds and hearts from being distracted by fear and worry. Better yet, give the wheel to GOD and let HIM drive. Ask HIM for help today! **Hebrews 13:5-6**

✝

Key Bible Verse

Hebrew 13:5-6 – "Keep your lives free from the love of money and be content with what you have, because God has said, "Never will I leave you; never will I forsake you." So we say with confidence, "The Lord is my helper; I will not be afraid. What can mere mortals do to me?"

Prayers & Notes

_____

_____

_____

_____

_____

_____

_____

A Blessing from Yesterday _____

Something I am Thankful for Today _____

March 22

What does average mean? It is the medium of a sum of numbers in math and can be misleading when used in personal comparisons. For example, there is no such thing as an average Christian. We are either Christians or we aren't. GOD sees each of us as equals, not averages. HE loves us all equally with all of HIS heart (**Romans 5:8**). Now is a good time to love GOD with all our hearts by loving others as JESUS did.

Key Bible Verse

Romans 5:8 – "But God demonstrates his own love for us in this: While we were still sinners, Christ died for us."

Prayers & Notes

_____

_____

_____

_____

_____

_____

_____

A Blessing from Yesterday _____

Something I am Thankful for Today _____

Patrick E. Moore

March 23

We are social beings. We desire our friends and family to be around us, and it can be difficult when they're not. The good news for Christians is that we know JESUS, and HE is around us 360 degrees. I heard and read lyrics from a new song from Heather Sorensen that says it all. "JESUS is in front of us, behind us, beside us to guide us, some things never change." Be comforted in that.

✝

Key Bible Verse

Psalm 19:1 – "The heavens declare the glory of God; the skies proclaim the work of his hands."

Prayers & Notes

_____

_____

_____

_____

_____

_____

_____

A Blessing from Yesterday _____

Something I am Thankful for Today _____

March 24

I like using power tools. However, regardless of my ability to use a tool, it needs power and will stop if the battery gets depleted. This reminds me that sometimes we need to recharge our spiritual batteries so GOD's power can work in our lives. JESUS' disciples learned twice they needed GOD's power to catch their fish, and without HIM, they caught nothing. **John 21:6-8.** Seek HIS Power and listen to where HE tells you to drop your nets.

Key Bible Verse

John 21:6 – "He said, throw your net on the right side of the boat and you will find some. When they did, they were unable to haul the net in because of the large number of fish."

Prayers & Notes

_____

_____

_____

_____

_____

_____

_____

A Blessing from Yesterday _____

Something I am Thankful for Today _____

March 25

I wondered what made up the roads and paths JESUS walked on over 2000 years ago. It was probably salt. It had small granules, was packed well and plentiful. It's estimated that JESUS Walked over 20,000 miles during his ministry. Wow, that's almost the equivalent of walking around the globe. Have you walked with HIM lately? Reach out. HE is always waiting to take your hand. **1 John 1:6-7.**

✝

Key Bible Verse

1 John 1:6-7 – "If we claim to have fellowship with him and yet walk in the darkness, we lie and do not live out the truth. But if we walk in the light, as he is in the light, we have fellowship with one another, and the blood of Jesus, his Son, purifies us from all sin."

Prayers & Notes

_____

_____

_____

_____

_____

A Blessing from Yesterday _____

Something I am Thankful for Today _____

March 26

I saw a beautiful picture this morning of clouds and blue skies. In the Bible, the word blue represents the heavens and God's word. **Exodus 24:10.** We need some blue skies in our life after some dreary days. Let the blue skies remind you of God and the blue skies promised ahead.

✝

Key Bible Verse

Exodus 24:10 – "and saw the God of Israel. Under his feet was something like a pavement made of lapis lazuli, as bright blue as the sky."

Prayers & Notes

_____

_____

_____

_____

_____

_____

_____

_____

_____

A Blessing from Yesterday _____

Something I am Thankful for Today _____

Patrick E. Moore

March 27

This morning I noticed the beauty of the English ivy that has clothed four large trees off my back porch. While beautiful, it is also choking the life out of the trees. Like ivy, sin sometimes creeps into our minds and lives to take hold and slowly chokes out our Christian witness. Beware, Satan is like a lion who comes to destroy (**1 Peter 5:8**). Stay in prayer and in GOD's WORD to prevent the thoughts of sin from taking root. Thank HIM today!

Key Bible Verse

1 Peter 5:8 – "Be alert and of sober mind. Your enemy the devil prowls around like a roaring lion looking for someone to devour."

Prayers & Notes

_____

_____

_____

_____

_____

_____

_____

A Blessing from Yesterday _____

Something I am Thankful for Today _____

March 28

The beginning of spring is exploding with color and new growth. The knockout roses have a reddish foliage indicating new buds of life are on the way. It's a reminder that the red blood of JESUS is what led to new life for you, me and all those who believe in HIM. Let the beautiful colors of spring remind you of your Heavenly FATHER today. **Matthew 6:28-30**

✝

Key Bible Verse

Matthew 6:28-29 - "And why do you worry about clothes? See how the flowers of the field grow. They do not labor or spin. Yet I tell you that not even Solomon in all his splendor was dressed like one of these"

Prayers & Notes

_____

_____

_____

_____

_____

_____

_____

A Blessing from Yesterday _____

Something I am Thankful for Today _____

Patrick E. Moore

March 29

A new interstellar comet has been discovered, meaning its orbit comes from outside our solar system. Do you know that there could be billions of solar systems? Wow. **Genesis 1:1** tells us that the heavens are what GOD created first. Ponder on the wonder and majesty of our GOD today. Fear not, worry not, GOD is in control. Trust HIM today!

✝

Key Bible Verse

Genesis 1:1 – "In the beginning God created the heavens and the earth."

Prayers & Notes

_____

_____

_____

_____

_____

_____

_____

_____

_____

A Blessing from Yesterday _____

Something I am Thankful for Today _____

March 30

"Koinonia" is a Greek word meaning fellowship and communion. Fellowship is to have something in common and to share. It's mentioned nineteen times in the Bible and is relevant to our Christian growth. It is simply loving and serving each other as CHRIST served HIS Disciples while "on earth" and does so for us from His throne in Heaven. **John 13:34-35.** Loving and serving are not components that are defined by time and distance. Love and serve daily.

✝

Key Bible Verse

John 13:34-35 - "A new command I give you: Love one another. As I have loved you, so you must love one another. By this everyone will know that you are my disciples, if you love one another."

Prayers & Notes

_____

_____

_____

_____

_____

_____

A Blessing from Yesterday _____

Something I am Thankful for Today _____

Patrick E. Moore

March 31

This is certainly a time when we need faith, right? And lots of it. Would you agree that we want the kind of faith JESUS had? Great. The good news is that we already have it. **Romans 12:3** says GOD gave us all a measure of Faith. What is a measure? Maybe it's all we need. Our job is to remove the fears, worry, sin behavior and unbelief to let the faith truly flow. Thank you, JESUS.

Key Bible Verse

Romans 12:3 – "For by the grace given me I say to every one of you: Do not think of yourself more highly than you ought, but rather think of yourself with sober judgment, in accordance with the faith God has distributed to each of you."

Prayers & Notes

_____

_____

_____

_____

_____

_____

A Blessing from Yesterday _____

Something I am Thankful for Today _____

April 1

Our lower bricks around our house have accumulated a lot of green discoloration from algae and moss, but yesterday I used my new pressure washer to remove it. It was amazing how clean and new the brick looked afterward. It reminded me of what GOD does with our sin when we confessed them to HIM: HE washes it away. **1 John 1:9**. Praise HIS Name forever!

✝

Key Bible Verse

1 John 1:9 – "If we confess our sins, he is faithful and just and will forgive us our sins and purify us from all unrighteousness."

Prayers & Notes

_____

_____

_____

_____

_____

_____

_____

A Blessing from Yesterday _____

Something I am Thankful for Today _____

Patrick E. Moore

April 2

In the 1970's, a struggling musician heard his dad tell him, "don't stop believing." Years later, he was a member of the popular rock band, Journey, and "Don't Stop Believing" became the title of one of the top rock tunes of all time. How true those words are for us today. In **Mark 9:23**, JESUS tells the father of a demon-possessed son, "everything is possible for one who believes." The father believed, and his son was healed. Don't stop believing!

✝

Key Bible Verse

Mark 9:23 - "'If you can?'" said Jesus. 'Everything is possible for one who believes.'"

Prayers & Notes

_____

_____

_____

_____

_____

_____

_____

A Blessing from Yesterday _____

Something I am Thankful for Today _____

April 3

A mountaintop is a physical location but also can describe a spiritual experience. It may not last long, but the images and memories can be lifelong and life changing. Read the mountaintop story in **Mark 9:2-5** when JESUS was transformed into dazzling white. HE took Peter, James and John to a mountaintop to renew their strength for the difficult days ahead. We certainly could use a spiritual mountaintop experience now, right? Keep praying.

Key Bible Verse

Mark 9:2-3 – "After six days Jesus took Peter, James and John with him and led them up a high mountain, where they were all alone. There he was transfigured before them. His clothes became dazzling white, whiter than anyone in the world could bleach them. "

Prayers & Notes

_____

_____

_____

_____

_____

_____

A Blessing from Yesterday _____

Something I am Thankful for Today _____

April 4

When I awoke this morning, it was still dark outside, and the streetlight in front of our house was still on, lighting the path for travelers on our road. It reminded me of **Psalms 119:105** which says GOD's WORD lights our path. Boy, is that something we need at this time. We are living in uncertain times, and with worry, fear and our daily sin, the path ahead appears foggy and impassable. Fear not, GOD is with us and will guide us through the darkness.

Key Bible Verse

Psalms 119:105 – "Your word is a lamp for my feet, a light on my path."

Prayers & Notes

_____

_____

_____

_____

_____

_____

_____

A Blessing from Yesterday _____

Something I am Thankful for Today _____

April 5

Today is Palm Sunday, and the first time I can remember that we will join the rest of the Christian world and worship from home due to the pandemic. Palm Sunday represents the triumphal entry of JESUS into Jerusalem before the crucifixion. "Blessed is the name of the LORD" (**Psalms 118.26**). Let's shout in a loud prayer of praise today for the King of Kings as the disciples did that day over 2000 years ago. Praise HIM today!

Key Bible Verse

Psalms 118.26 – "Blessed is he who comes in the name of the LORD. From the house of the LORD we bless you."

Prayers & Notes

_____

_____

_____

_____

_____

_____

_____

A Blessing from Yesterday _____

Something I am Thankful for Today _____

Patrick E. Moore

April 6

Ever called anybody out by name for doing something bad? Did you know that, as Christians, we are to call out by name what is ailing us, and demand it leave us, in JESUS Name. **Philippians 2:10.** Whether it's a virus, cancer, shame, guilt, worry, etc., it must bow before the name of JESUS. Let's use this HOLY week to kick some evil out of our bodies and out of the ones we love. Thank HIM for that power.

Key Bible Verse

Philippians 2:10 – "that at the name of Jesus every knee should bow, in heaven and on earth and under the earth"

Prayers & Notes

_____

_____

_____

_____

_____

_____

_____

A Blessing from Yesterday _____

Something I am Thankful for Today _____

April 7

Ever ridden a really big, old, wooden, fast rollercoaster? It can be scary, but at least you know the ride will be over in a few minutes. You could say everything about the last month has been like a roller coaster, but the ride may not end soon. Our emotions, the news, and the stock market have been up, down and downright scary. Here is the advice. Ready? Remember, JESUS is always near, so at times like this, hold on tight to HIM! **Joshua 23:8**

Key Bible Verse

Joshua 23:8 – "But you are to hold fast to the LORD your God, as you have until now."

Prayers & Notes

_____

_____

_____

_____

_____

_____

_____

A Blessing from Yesterday _____

Something I am Thankful for Today _____

Patrick E. Moore

April 8

We have a flowering tree in our yard that started blooming over the last few days. It's a dogwood tree with white, beautiful petals. Dogwood trees bloom around Easter every year, and the petals are shaped like crosses, reminding us of the cross as we celebrate Easter. This week let the blooming dogwoods remind you of JESUS on the cross, and remember, we must each take up our cross daily and follow HIM. **Luke 9:23**.

Key Bible Verse

Luke 9:23 – "Then he said to them all: "Whoever wants to be my disciple must deny themselves and take up their cross daily and follow me.""

Prayers & Notes

_____

_____

_____

_____

_____

_____

_____

A Blessing from Yesterday _____

Something I am Thankful for Today _____

April 9

Do you know some people who always seem to have joy in their hearts, regardless of the circumstance? Sure, we all do, and we should strive to be like them. Here is the good news. GOD didn't make us that way. No, there are no default settings for joy, love, hate, hope, etc. GOD made us in such a way to choose those things. Want joy? Ask GOD for it! Your joy is a choice. **Romans 15:13**.

Key Bible Verse

Romans 15:13 – "May the God of hope fill you with all joy and peace as you trust in him, so that you may overflow with hope by the power of the Holy Spirit."

Prayers & Notes

_____

_____

_____

_____

_____

_____

_____

A Blessing from Yesterday _____

Something I am Thankful for Today _____

April 10

Yesterday was Maundy Thursday commemorating the Last Supper. Our Sunday School class celebrated it last night with communion via a Zoom meeting. I will never forget it and hope we do every year. The sacraments represent the blood and body of JESUS who came as the unblemished lamb sacrifice for our sins. **Luke 22:19** says "this is my body given for you, do this in remembrance of me."

✝

Key Bible Verse

Luke 22:19 – "And he took bread, gave thanks and broke it, and gave it to them, saying, this is my body given for you; do this in remembrance of me.'"

Prayers & Notes

_____

_____

_____

_____

_____

_____

_____

A Blessing from Yesterday _____

Something I am Thankful for Today _____

April 11

I was posed a great question yesterday by a Spiritual mentor of mine, and it was "Why did GOD make man on the sixth day and then rest on the seventh day?" It was the 7th day because GOD was preparing man for everything he would ever need (**Genesis 1-2**). GOD created us in HIS image, rested and declared it good. Don't be worried about today or tomorrow, because GOD has prepared a way with everything we will ever need. Trust HIM!

Key Bible Verse

Genesis 2:2-3 – "By the seventh day God had finished the work he had been doing; so on the seventh day he rested from all his work. Then God blessed the seventh day and made it holy, because on it he rested from all the work of creating that he had done."

Prayers & Notes

_____

_____

_____

_____

_____

A Blessing from Yesterday _____

Something I am Thankful for Today _____

April 12

Easter is the day we celebrate that JESUS arose from the tomb after dying on a cross for the sins of all humanity. Without the Resurrection, we have no Christian Faith, but because of it, we have Faith. Yes, JESUS returned to Heaven not to desert us but to guide us. For those who know HIM, HE left us a Blessing that will never leave us. Worship HIM with joy and serve HIM with gladness. HE has Risen indeed! **Matthew 28:6**

Key Bible Verse

Matthew 28:6 – "He is not here; he has risen, just as he said. Come and see the place where he lay."

Prayers & Notes

_____

_____

_____

_____

_____

_____

_____

_____

A Blessing from Yesterday _____

Something I am Thankful for Today _____

April 13

Missouri's nickname is "the show me state," basically saying don't tell me, show me. This is not a new concept. After the Resurrection, many of Jesus' Disciples had doubt until they saw HIM or touched HIM. Those disciples needed that physical proof, and it supercharged their faith to live and die spreading the GOOD NEWS. According to John's account, JESUS said "Blessed are those who have not seen and yet have believed." **John 20:29**. Have Faith!

✝

Key Bible Verse

John 20:29 – "Then Jesus told him, "Because you have seen me, you have believed; blessed are those who have not seen and yet have believed."

Prayers & Notes

_____

_____

_____

_____

_____

_____

A Blessing from Yesterday _____

Something I am Thankful for Today _____

April 14

Ever hear about Fuller's Soap or Fuller's Field? In ancient Syria, the meaning of full was "to whiten." A fuller used a harsh soap and washed and beat the cloth until it was clean and white. It's a dirty job. In **Mark 9:3**, the writer says JESUS' clothes became radiant and whiter than any fuller could make them. The same is true of our sins when we follow JESUS. HE takes our dirty sins and makes them white as snow. Thank HIM Today!

✝

Key Bible Verse

Mark 9:3 – "His clothes became dazzling white, whiter than anyone in the world could bleach them."

Prayers & Notes

_____

_____

_____

_____

_____

_____

_____

A Blessing from Yesterday _____

Something I am Thankful for Today _____

April 15

In 1953, Rocket Chemical Company worked on formulating a water displacement product. On the 40th attempt, they succeeded in creating a popular product, WD-40. In the Bible, the number 40 has great significance as a period of testing, trial or probation followed by a new beginning. Today, we hear the word quarantine a lot, and it also means 40 days. Hmmm... I think GOD has a new beginning in mind for us today. Trust HIM.

Key Bible Verse

Exodus 24:18 – "then Moses entered the cloud as he went on up the mountain. And he stayed on the mountain forty days and forty nights."

Prayers & Notes

_____

_____

_____

_____

_____

_____

_____

A Blessing from Yesterday _____

Something I am Thankful for Today _____

Patrick E. Moore

April 16

Ever heard of a coping saw? It's a small handsaw carpenters use to delicately cut (cope) wood trim to fit together in a nice seam. JESUS was a carpenter, and through his teaching and HIS WORD, he shows us how to cope with the daily, difficult and trying issues of life. Let HIM trim away our fear, guilt, and anxiety so we can see HIM clearly in everything we think, see and do! **Jeremiah 29:11**.

Key Bible Verse

Jeremiah 29:11 – "For I know the plans I have for you," Remember the LORD, "plans to prosper you and not to harm you, plans to give you hope and a future."

Prayers & Notes

_____

_____

_____

_____

_____

_____

_____

A Blessing from Yesterday _____

Something I am Thankful for Today _____

April 17

It was chilly this morning as I stood in my driveway and shared my daily prayer time with my Heavenly FATHER. When I opened my eyes, a burst of sunlight splattered through the trees and made me smile. No doubt it was a "GOD wink." It reminded me that GOD's light gives hope to our hearts when we need it, warmth to our soul when it's cold, and light in a world full of darkness. Praise HIM today. **Isaiah 9:2**.

Key Bible Verse

Isaiah 9:2 – "The people walking in darkness have seen a great light; on those living in the land of deep darkness a light has dawned."

Prayers & Notes

_____

_____

_____

_____

_____

_____

A Blessing from Yesterday _____

Something I am Thankful for Today _____

Patrick E. Moore

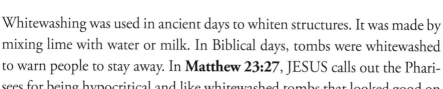

April 18

Whitewashing was used in ancient days to whiten structures. It was made by mixing lime with water or milk. In Biblical days, tombs were whitewashed to warn people to stay away. In **Matthew 23:27**, JESUS calls out the Pharisees for being hypocritical and like whitewashed tombs that looked good on the outside but contained death on the inside. Read GOD's WORD today so HE can paint you with HIS Glory on the inside and out.

✝

Key Bible Verse

Matthew 23:27 - "Woe to you, teachers of the law and Pharisees, you hypocrites! You are like whitewashed tombs, which look beautiful on the outside but on the inside are full of the bones of the dead and everything unclean."

Prayers & Notes

_____

_____

_____

_____

_____

_____

_____

A Blessing from Yesterday _____

Something I am Thankful for Today _____

April 19

A hypocrite may say heshe is praying for a miracle when he isn't (i.e., praying for a cure during a pandemic) and blasphemy might insult GOD and not give HIM credit when the miracle comes true (i.e. Ignore GOD's involvement or give credit elsewhere) My prayer is that we all will earnestly pray together and then praise GOD for the outcome. **Matthew 12:31-32.** Seek HIM today!

✝

Key Bible Verse

Matthew 12:31-32 – "And so I tell you, every kind of sin and slander can be forgiven, but blasphemy against the Spirit will not be forgiven. Anyone who speaks a word against the Son of Man will be forgiven, but anyone who speaks against the Holy Spirit will not be forgiven, either in this age or in the age to come."

Prayers & Notes

_____

_____

_____

_____

_____

_____

A Blessing from Yesterday _____

Something I am Thankful for Today _____

Patrick E. Moore

April 20

Think about the great explorers of our time. They travelled to unknown places for unknown periods of time. What faith and courage they must have had. Could you do it? Abraham was the original explorer, and the book of Genesis tells his story. He was a righteous man and became the author of our faith. We must have Faith to travel to the unknown with GOD. It could be a long journey, but HE promises us a glorious resting place. **John 14:1-4**

✝

Key Bible Verse

John 14:1-4 – "Do not let your hearts be troubled. You believe in God; believe also in me. My Father's house has many rooms; if that were not so, would I have told you that I am going there to prepare a place for you? And if I go and prepare a place for you, I will come back and take you to be with me that you also may be where I am. You know the way to the place where I am going."

Prayers & Notes

_____

_____

_____

_____

_____

A Blessing from Yesterday _____

Something I am Thankful for Today _____

April 21

Sometimes the best medicine for improving your mood from stress and anxiety is to find a quiet place outside, be still and just listen. Research says it is a great exercise for improving your mood. This morning while sitting still outside, I have identified dozens of different sounds including birds chirping and singing, the wind blowing through the trees, and even distant airplane hums and train whistles. A Bible verse comes to mind: "Be still, and know I am GOD." **Psalms 46:10-11.** Thank HIM today!

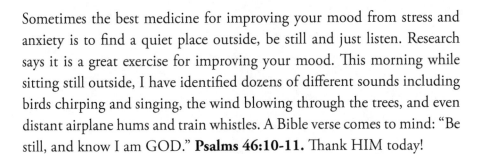

Key Bible Verse

Psalms 46:10-11 – "He says, "Be still, and know that I am God; I will be exalted among the nations, I will be exalted in the earth. The Lord Almighty is with us; the God of Jacob is our fortress."

Prayers & Notes

_____

_____

_____

_____

_____

_____

_____

A Blessing from Yesterday _____

Something I am Thankful for Today _____

April 22

The deep cut lines in your concrete driveway are called expansion joints. Concrete expands and contracts, and it is always under stress. The expansion joints prevent cracking and keep water from eroding the concrete from within. We need to build expansion joints in life's foundation to prevent our faith from cracking or eroding under stress. Reading GOD's WORD daily is my expansion joint for my faith. Try it. **Joshua 1:9**

Key Bible Verse

Joshua 1:9 – "Have I not commanded you? Be strong and courageous. Do not be afraid; do not be discouraged, for the LORD your God will be with you wherever you go."

Prayers & Notes

_____

_____

_____

_____

_____

_____

_____

A Blessing from Yesterday _____

Something I am Thankful for Today _____

April 23

Are you happy and full of joy? Great! If you aren't, why not? Are happiness and joy the same thing? No. Happiness comes from "happenings." Joy comes from the LORD and does not rely on what is happening. **John 15:11**. Some people do seem genetically predisposed to being happy and positive, but when you receive your joy from GOD, being happy and positive will come along for the ride. Receiving joy is not a lottery pick, it is available to everyone. Seek your joy today!

Key Bible Verse

John 15:11 – "I have told you this so that my joy may be in you and that your joy may be complete."

Prayers & Notes

_____

_____

_____

_____

_____

_____

_____

A Blessing from Yesterday _____

Something I am Thankful for Today _____

April 24

The paper clip was patented in 1867 with many different designs to follow. The most popular design was and is the gem clip that was developed in 1892 by a company in New York City but never patented. The paper clip replaced the straight pin that was used to hold papers together. Sometimes life gets crazy, and we need something to hold us together. Seek GOD. HE can hold anything together. **Colossians 1:17**

Key Bible Verse

Colossians 1:17 – "He is before all things, and in him all things hold together."

Prayers & Notes

_____

_____

_____

_____

_____

_____

_____

A Blessing from Yesterday _____

Something I am Thankful for Today _____

April 25

This morning, the water from the early morning rain beaded up on the recently sealed and waterproofed wooden deck. The seal repels the water and protects and preserves the wood. That's a great analogy for us as Christians. We know that GOD, through the HOLY SPIRIT, promises to protect and seal our hearts and souls from evil. **Psalms 121:7**. Let GOD apply or renew the waterproofing of your soul today. Amen.

Key Bible Verse

Psalms 121:7 – "The LORD will keep you from all harm—he will watch over your life"

Prayers & Notes

_____

_____

_____

_____

_____

_____

_____

A Blessing from Yesterday _____

Something I am Thankful for Today _____

Patrick E. Moore

April 26

There is a gentle wind blowing this morning. Even though I cannot see or hear It, I can feel it on my face and see it moving the leaves on the trees. In **John 3:8**, JESUS says "the wind blows where it wishes and so do those that are born of the Spirit." The Greek word for "wind" is the same as the word for "spirit." Being born again in CHRIST comes from GOD, and like the wind, we will be known as HIS by what people see in us. Praise HIM today!

✝

Key Bible Verse

John 3:8 – "The wind blows wherever it pleases. You hear its sound, but you cannot tell where it comes from or where it is going. So it is with everyone born of the Spirit."

Prayers & Notes

_____

_____

_____

_____

_____

_____

_____

A Blessing from Yesterday _____

Something I am Thankful for Today _____

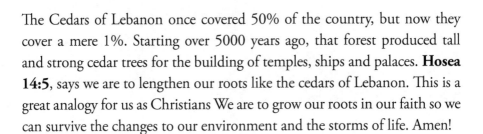

April 27

The Cedars of Lebanon once covered 50% of the country, but now they cover a mere 1%. Starting over 5000 years ago, that forest produced tall and strong cedar trees for the building of temples, ships and palaces. **Hosea 14:5**, says we are to lengthen our roots like the cedars of Lebanon. This is a great analogy for us as Christians We are to grow our roots in our faith so we can survive the changes to our environment and the storms of life. Amen!

✝

Key Bible Verse

Hosea 14:5 – "I will be like the dew to Israel; he will blossom like a lily. Like a cedar of Lebanon he will send down his roots"

Prayers & Notes

_____

_____

_____

_____

_____

_____

_____

A Blessing from Yesterday _____

Something I am Thankful for Today _____

April 28

We have a "Porch Rules" sign on our back porch, and one of the ten rules is the word "Relax." That word is of Greek origin from the 15th century and means "to loosen or make less tense. "A good example of that concept can be found in **Psalms 116:5-7** where it says, "return to your rest, my soul." The author, likely King David, tells us to "return" our souls to rest because GOD has been good to us. As you go through this day, let your soul rest. GOD is with you.

Key Bible Verse

Psalms 116:7 – "Return to your rest, my soul, for the Lord has been good to you."

Prayers & Notes

_____

_____

_____

_____

_____

_____

_____

A Blessing from Yesterday _____

Something I am Thankful for Today _____

April 29

While visiting friends in the country a few days ago, we saw a beautiful coyote standing at the edge of a tree line at the top of a hill. Coyotes have been in North America longer than man. Its predators are the wolf and man. Don't you long for a time when there will be peace with no predators or enemies? **Isaiah 65:25** says that there will be a time again where the wolf will eat with the lamb. Keep praying for that day.

✝

Key Bible Verse

Isaiah 65:25 – "The wolf and the lamb will feed together, and the lion will eat straw like the ox, and dust will be the serpent's food. They will neither harm nor destroy on all my holy mountain, says the LORD."

Prayers & Notes

_____

_____

_____

_____

_____

_____

_____

A Blessing from Yesterday _____

Something I am Thankful for Today _____

April 30

Gates come in all shapes and sizes and are opened by a latch of some sort. They also may be locked to keep people out. The "Pearly Gates of Heaven" is an informal name for the gateway to Heaven described in **Revelation 21:21**. That is the gate I am excited about. Heaven is the dwelling place of GOD and the New Jerusalem. My prayer today is that we will all meet at that Heavenly Gate. How? Read **Romans 10:9-10.**

✝

Key Bible Verse

Romans 10:9-10 – "If you declare with your mouth, 'Jesus is Lord,' and believe in your heart that God raised him from the dead, you will be saved. For it is with your heart that you believe and are justified, and it is with your mouth that you profess your faith and are saved."

Prayers & Notes

_____

_____

_____

_____

_____

_____

A Blessing from Yesterday _____

Something I am Thankful for Today _____

May 1

The flowering honeysuckle in our yard reminds me of visiting Pappy and Granny's farm when I was a boy. We used to pinch off the flowers and sip the sweet nectar from the petals. It's interesting how fragrances and tastes trigger our memories. In **Psalms 119:103**, David writes of the sweet taste of GOD's WORDS as sweeter than honey. A daily dose of HIS sweetness is a great way to start the day. May you taste HIS WORDS today.

✝

Key Bible Verse

Psalms 119:103 – "How sweet are your words to my taste, sweeter than honey to my mouth!"

Prayers & Notes

_____

_____

_____

_____

_____

_____

_____

A Blessing from Yesterday _____

Something I am Thankful for Today _____

Patrick E. Moore

May 2

A beautiful day on the golf course yesterday was great for my psyche after a quarantine. I hit some good shots but also lost two balls in water hazards. Boy, life can be like that sometimes. You have a nice round of life going, hitting great, but then the winds of life blow you into a hazard. **Isaiah 43:18-19** says don't ponder the past, because GOD has got something great in store for us. Maybe a birdie on 18 in Heaven.

Key Bible Verse

Isaiah 43:18-19 - "Forget the former things; do not dwell on the past. See, I am doing a new thing! Now it springs up; do you not perceive it? I am making a way in the wilderness and streams in the wasteland."

Prayers & Notes

_____

_____

_____

_____

_____

_____

_____

A Blessing from Yesterday _____

Something I am Thankful for Today _____

May 3

Do you have everything you need for the next 40 days? You probably don't, and neither did Moses as He led GOD's people out of Egypt. How could He plan for 2000 tons of food, 4000 tons of firewood, and 11 million gallons of water EACH DAY? He didn't. Moses trusted GOD. Shouldn't we trust GOD for what we need each day? **Matthew 6:25** is a simple verse that reminds us GOD will provide everything we need. Trust HIM!

Key Bible Verse

Matthew 6:25 - "Therefore I tell you, do not worry about your life, what you will eat or drink; or about your body, what you will wear. Is not life more than food, and the body more than clothes?"

Prayers & Notes

_____

_____

_____

_____

_____

_____

_____

A Blessing from Yesterday _____

Something I am Thankful for Today _____

Patrick E. Moore

May 4

A powerful storm knocked out our electricity last night. We went to bed in the darkness, not knowing when the power would come back on. It reminded me that the Bible talks about those people who are in the darkness because they haven't heard or have chosen not to accept JESUS as the CHRIST. The good news is the Bible mentions "Light" more than darkness, and you can choose to walk in the light. **Acts 26:18**. Come to HIS Light today!

Key Bible Verse

Acts 26:18 – "to open their eyes and turn them from darkness to light, and from the power of Satan to God, so that they may receive forgiveness of sins and a place among those who are sanctified by faith in me."

Prayers & Notes

_____

_____

_____

_____

_____

_____

_____

A Blessing from Yesterday _____

Something I am Thankful for Today _____

No Mountain Too High   125

May 5

How did you get to where you are at this moment? Are you blessed beyond your understanding? Of course, your faithfulness or lack of will have an impact, but maybe you have stepped into a generational blessing. A faithful father, praying grandmother, or others in the generations before you played a part. It started with Abraham.

Genesis 12:2-3. Embrace the blessing and pass it on for future generations.

Key Bible Verse

Genesis 12:2-3 - "I will make you into a great nation, and I will bless you; I will make your name great, and you will be a blessing. I will bless those who bless you, and whoever curses you I will curse; and all peoples on earth will be blessed through you."

Prayers & Notes

_____

_____

_____

_____

_____

A Blessing from Yesterday _____

Something I am Thankful for Today _____

May 6

My laptop stopped working when we lost power from a storm, and it wouldn't come back on. I prayed for an easy fix, and the technician took off the cover, took out the battery, plugged it back in, and it started working again. Sometimes during the storms of life, our batteries run down, too, and we don't just need rest, we need to disconnect from the result of the storm and let GOD's WORD reconnect our souls to HIM. **Psalms 139:23-24.**

✝

Key Bible Verse

Psalms 139:23-24 – "Search me, God, and know my heart; test me and know my anxious thoughts. See if there is any offensive way in me and lead me in the way everlasting."

Prayers & Notes

_____

_____

_____

_____

_____

_____

A Blessing from Yesterday _____

Something I am Thankful for Today _____

May 7

Railroad ties were first used in England and were originally called "sleepers," an old carpentry term for timber lying on its widest side "at rest." The rails are secured with spikes, so the train won't come off the tracks. Do you ever think your family and life are about to come off the tracks because of tough times? When things get shaky, turn to GOD's WORD and let the HOLY SPIRIT keep you on the tracks. **Psalms 23:3**.

✝

Key Bible Verse

Psalms 23:3 – "He refreshes my soul. He guides me along the right paths for his name's sake."

Prayers & Notes

_____

_____

_____

_____

_____

_____

_____

A Blessing from Yesterday _____

Something I am Thankful for Today _____

Patrick E. Moore

May 8

The game "Tic Tac Toe" is called "Naught and Crosses" in England and has been played the same since the early 1800's. Our Christian journey is like a big game of Naught and Crosses. Think about it. GOD gives us supernatural powers to defeat Satan (**2 Corinthians 10:4-5**). When Satan tempts us, he enters a naught on the board, and when we seek GOD and HIS WORD, a cross goes on the board. With GOD's help, we win every time!

Key Bible Verse

2 Corinthians 10:4-5 – "The weapons we fight with are not the weapons of the world. On the contrary, they have divine power to demolish strongholds. We demolish arguments and every pretension that sets itself up against the knowledge of God, and we take captive every thought to make it obedient to Christ."

Prayers & Notes

_____

_____

_____

_____

_____

A Blessing from Yesterday _____

Something I am Thankful for Today _____

May 9

"Take Ten" is a term that means to take a break, i.e., 10 minutes. Ten is used as a perfect score in some sports like gymnastics or figure skating. It is also mentioned 242 times in the Bible. GOD obviously thought it was an important number when HE gave MOSES the Ten Commandments. Some Biblical scholars say it is one of GOD's perfect number, one of divine perfection. "Take Ten" with GOD today!

Key Bible Verse

Exodus 34:28 – "Moses was there with the LORD forty days and forty nights without eating bread or drinking water. And he wrote on the tablets the words of the covenant—the Ten Commandments."

Prayers & Notes

_____

_____

_____

_____

_____

_____

_____

A Blessing from Yesterday _____

Something I am Thankful for Today _____

Patrick E. Moore

May 10

Is something missing in your life that you wish GOD would provide? Have you asked HIM? Why not? The Prayer of Jabez is the title of a book based on **1 Chronicles 4:9-10.** It is about a man who asked for GOD's blessing, and it was given to him. This book was a life changer for me 25 years ago. **James 4:2** basically says, "you have not because you ask not." Don't hesitate, ask GOD for your desires today!

Key Bible Verse

I Chronicles 4:9-10 – "Jabez was more honorable than his brothers. His mother had named him Jabez, saying, "I gave birth to him in pain." Jabez cried out to the God of Israel, "Oh, that you would bless me and enlarge my territory! Let your hand be with me and keep me from harm so that I will be free from pain." And God granted his request."

Prayers & Notes

_____

_____

_____

_____

_____

A Blessing from Yesterday _____

Something I am Thankful for Today _____

May 11

A hinge is a bearing that connects two hard objects allowing them to open and shut without coming apart. The metal versions go back to the bronze days. We all have dozens in our home on doors and cabinets. The HOLY SPIRIT is like the hinge on the doors of life that open and close regularly so there must be some hinges involved. My prayer is you will walk through the doors the HOLY SPIRIT opens for you today!

Key Bible Verse

Revelation 3:7-8 - "And to the angel of the church in Philadelphia write: He who is holy, who is true, who has the key of David, who opens, and no one will shut, and who shuts, and no one opens, says this: 'I know your deeds. Behold, I have put before you an open door which no one can shut, because you have a little power, and have kept My word, and have not denied My name."

Prayers & Notes

_____

_____

_____

_____

_____

A Blessing from Yesterday _____

Something I am Thankful for Today _____

Patrick E. Moore

May 12

~

Routine is a habit or sequence that comes from the French word "route." We all have routines. GOD inspired "My Daily Healing Thought" as a routine for me over 500 days ago after I received an unexpected and frightening diagnosis. I committed to learn about GOD's healing power and share it with others. I have learned that the heart, mind and soul are all connected to healing, which starts with loving GOD. **Matthew 22:37**. Thank You FATHER.

Key Bible Verse

Matthew 22:37 - Jesus replied: "'Love the Lord your God with all your heart and with all your soul and with all your mind.'"

Prayers & Notes

_____

_____

_____

_____

_____

_____

_____

A Blessing from Yesterday _____

Something I am Thankful for Today _____

May 13

As Christians, we all believe in Heaven as our eternal resting place and that there will be perfect harmony, joy, and peace forever there, right? Is it possible to experience some of that harmony, joy and peace now? Yes, read the Lord 's Prayer in **Matthew 6:9-13** and notice "HIS Kingdom come; thy will be done on earth as it is in HEAVEN." You can have that peace and joy now by being in the presence of the LORD. Praise HIM today!

✝

Key Bible Verse

Matthew 6:10 – "your kingdom come, your will be done, on earth as it is in heaven."

Prayers & Notes

_____

_____

_____

_____

_____

_____

A Blessing from Yesterday _____

Something I am Thankful for Today _____

May 14

~

Pillars are used in construction to beautify and support a structure, but in the Bible, they are used in a variety of ways. The pillar of fire was how GOD led Moses and the Jews during the exodus, the pillar of salt was the punishment for Lot's wife for disobeying GOD, and a pillar of rocks was used to memorialize GOD's works or promises. GOD's WORD is the pillar of our faith and the bridge between Heaven and Earth. **Revelation 3:12.**

Key Bible Verse

Revelation 3:12 – "The one who is victorious I will make a pillar in the temple of my God. Never again will they leave it. I will write on them the name of my God and the name of the city of my God, the new Jerusalem, which is coming down out of heaven from my God; and I will also write on them my new name."

Prayers & Notes

_____

_____

_____

_____

_____

_____

A Blessing from Yesterday _____

Something I am Thankful for Today _____

May 15

A Hope or Dowry Chest is a piece of furniture that was first used in 9th- century Egypt. It was traditionally used by unmarried women to collect household items and clothing as they anticipated married life. Thank goodness, as Christians, we don't need a chest to carry our hope in. The hope we have in Christ JESUS is in our hearts and minds. **Jeremiah 29:11**. Need a little hope today? Seek your Heavenly FATHER in prayer!

Key Bible Verse

Jeremiah 29:11 – "For I know the plans I have for you," Declares the LORD, "plans to prosper you and not to harm you, plans to give you hope and a future."

Prayers & Notes

_____

_____

_____

_____

_____

_____

_____

A Blessing from Yesterday _____

Something I am Thankful for Today _____

May 16

Do you like to walk barefooted in the grass or on the beach? I sure do. Walking barefoot is mentioned once in the Old Testament and once in the New Testament where GOD instructed those in HIS presence to walk barefooted because they were walking on HOLY Ground. What made the ground Holy was the presence of GOD. Here is the Good News: for those who know HIM, HIS Presence is with us always. Walk barefooted with HIM today!

Key Bible Verse

Acts 7:33 – "Then the Lord said to him, 'Take off your sandals, for the place where you are standing is holy ground.'"

Prayers & Notes

_____

_____

_____

_____

_____

_____

_____

A Blessing from Yesterday _____

Something I am Thankful for Today _____

May 17

I just bought an electronic device to boost the Wi-Fi signal to our new garage office, and it works great. It provides a good analogy for how GOD used HIS disciples after HIS resurrection. He plugged them in to Jerusalem, Damascus, Antioch, Asia Minor, Greece and finally Rome. That's what GOD does when we are obedient to HIS WORD. HE will plug us in to people and places to boost the Gospel. Amen!

Key Bible Verse

Exodus 19:5 - "Now if you obey me fully and keep my covenant, then out of all nations you will be my treasured possession. Although the whole earth is mine,"

Prayers & Notes

_____

_____

_____

_____

_____

_____

_____

A Blessing from Yesterday _____

Something I am Thankful for Today _____

Patrick E. Moore

May 18

In business negotiations, you bring your assets and liabilities to the table looking for a deal. When you get to know JESUS, what you bring to the table" is something difficult. JESUS calls us to bring only our liabilities to HIS table of redemption such as our sin, our fear, our shame, our hurt and our doubt. By HIS Blood, HE will remove those things from our lives forever. Bring it all to HIS Table today! **1 John 1:19.**

Key Bible Verse

1 John.1:9 – "If we confess our sins, he is faithful and just and will forgive us our sins and purify us from all unrighteousness."

Prayers & Notes

_____

_____

_____

_____

_____

_____

_____

A Blessing from Yesterday _____

Something I am Thankful for Today _____

May 19

As I was repairing this birdhouse so I could stand it back up in the yard, I started thinking about birds and what we can learn from them. First thing in the morning, I hear them chirping and singing to each other. I love that they seem cheerful and thankful that God provides food and shelter every day. It was interesting to learn that birds are mentioned over 300 times in the Bible, but my favorite verses that mention birds are **Matthew 6:25-28**. What a great lesson for us. Don't worry; God will provide what we need each day. Amen

✝

Key Bible Verse

Matthew 6:26 – "Look at the birds of the air; they do not sow or reap or store away in barns, and yet your heavenly Father feeds them. Are you not much more valuable than they?"

Prayers & Notes

_____

_____

_____

_____

_____

A Blessing from Yesterday _____

Something I am Thankful for Today _____

Patrick E. Moore

May 20

I saw a measuring cup on the kitchen counter this morning and remembered Karen using it for measuring ingredients in a bowl. Each recipe requires a certain measure of ingredients. The measuring cup made me think of our faith because Paul says in **Romans 12:3** that we are all given a measure of faith by God, and all gifts are given in grace. Thank Him today for that faith and for your gifts and use them to glorify Him.

Key Bible Verse

Romans 12:3 – "For by the grace given me I say to every one of you: Do not think of yourself more highly than you ought, but rather think of yourself with sober judgment, in accordance with the faith God has distributed to each of you."

Prayers & Notes

_____

_____

_____

_____

_____

_____

A Blessing from Yesterday _____

Something I am Thankful for Today _____

May 21

The term "all in" means betting all your chips in Texas poker. Webster's says it means "fully committed." As Christians, we know that GOD the FATHER is fully committed to each of us, and that's why HE sent HIS son JESUS to die for our sins. The real question is "are you and I fully committed to HIM?" What would the world look like if we were? Don't play it safe, it only leads to regrets. Go "all in" for CHRIST TODAY!

Key Bible Verse

Matthew 16:3 – "Commit to the LORD whatever you do, and he will establish your plans."

Prayers & Notes

_____

_____

_____

_____

_____

_____

_____

A Blessing from Yesterday _____

Something I am Thankful for Today _____

May 22

"Going on a wild goose chase" means pursuing something unlikely to be caught as a wild goose. The phrase arrived in our language in the 1700's and refers to "wasting time." The Bible has something to say to us about wasting time. Read **Ephesians 5:15-17**. Note it says, "making the best use of our time combined with the will of GOD." Don't spend your time on things that don't bring glory to HIS Name, and you will stop wasting time.

✝

Key Bible Verse

Ephesians 5:15-17 – "Be very careful, then, how you live—not as unwise but as wise, making the most of every opportunity, because the days are evil. Therefore do not be foolish but understand what the Lord's will is."

Prayers & Notes

_____

_____

_____

_____

_____

_____

_____

A Blessing from Yesterday _____

Something I am Thankful for Today _____

May 23

A threshold is an entrance or doorway, and we cross through them all day long. A Spiritual threshold is quite different, because it can lead to a spiritual breakthrough. Always standing in the way will be Satan, who will try to intimidate, scare or discourage us in some way. The Good News is, with GOD's Power, we can push through any struggle into victory. **Psalms 44:5**. Cross the threshold into GOD's Kingdom today.

✝

Key Bible Verse

Psalms 44:5 – "Through you we push back our enemies; through your name we trample our foes."

Prayers & Notes

_____

_____

_____

_____

_____

_____

A Blessing from Yesterday _____

Something I am Thankful for Today _____

May 24

If you buy something mechanical or electrical, it usually comes with a warranty from the manufacturer. If it breaks within the warranty period, the company will fix or repair the item at no charge. Where do we go for a broken heart or tarnished soul? Go to your Heavenly FATHER, the maker of Heaven and Earth. HE provides an eternal warranty, with no cost, no paperwork and no hassle. Call HIM in prayer today!

✝

Key Bible Verse

Psalm 34:18 – "The LORD is close to the brokenhearted and saves those who are crushed in spirit."

Prayers & Notes

_____

_____

_____

_____

_____

_____

_____

A Blessing from Yesterday _____

Something I am Thankful for Today _____

May 25

Ever been on a long and winding drive on bad roads? Sure, you have. Sometimes the roads we travel in life seems that way, bumpy, with detours and potholes along the way. In **Isaiah 42:16**, it says HE who will come will make the crooked roads straight. That's not talking about removing obstacles or making the journey easier in life. It is talking about our hearts and making them right with GOD. Let's align our HEARTS with GOD today!

✝

Key Bible Verse

Isaiah 42:16 – "I will lead the blind by ways they have not known, along unfamiliar paths I will guide them; I will turn the darkness into light before them and make the rough places smooth. These are the things I will do; I will not forsake them."

Prayers & Notes

_____

_____

_____

_____

_____

A Blessing from Yesterday _____

Something I am Thankful for Today _____

Patrick E. Moore

May 26

Wood decays and rots because of the presence of moisture and fungi. Moral or spiritual decay is the opposite. It occurs because of the absence of something essential – GOD. They both can occur from the inside out. Therefore, just as we might repair and weatherproof new wood, we need to repair our spiritual brokenness and decay-proof our society and families by adding more of GOD's word into our lives. **Psalms 16:10**

Key Bible Verse

Psalms 16:10 – "because you will not abandon me to the realm of the dead, nor will you let your faithful one sees Decay."

Prayers & Notes

_____

_____

_____

_____

_____

_____

_____

A Blessing from Yesterday _____

Something I am Thankful for Today _____

May 27

I woke up thinking about date, subject and title, which are parts of a formal business letter. It was a little odd, because I don't write many formal letters anymore, so maybe GOD wanted me to share it as a prayer template. The date should be today and every day, the subject should be thankfulness, and the title would be Heavenly FATHER. Start there, and then share your heart. **Philippians 4:6**. Amen.

Key Bible Verse

Philippians 4:6 – "Do not be anxious about anything, but in every situation, by prayer and petition, with thanksgiving, present your requests to God."

Prayers & Notes

_____

_____

_____

_____

_____

_____

_____

A Blessing from Yesterday _____

Something I am Thankful for Today _____

Patrick E. Moore

May 28

"Dependent" is a noun or adjective, but often our culture sees the word as weak. Therefore, it promotes and pushes for independence from everything and everybody, including GOD. To me, it is very presumptuous to assume we don't need anyone, especially GOD. That is arrogance and pride. My prayer is that you and I can grow and mature into dependence on GOD for everything. **Proverbs 3:5-6**. Lean on HIM today!

Key Bible Verse

Proverbs 3:5-6 – "Trust in the LORD with all your heart and lean not on your own understanding; in all your ways submit to him, and he will make your paths straight."

Prayers & Notes

_____

_____

_____

_____

_____

_____

_____

A Blessing from Yesterday _____

Something I am Thankful for Today _____

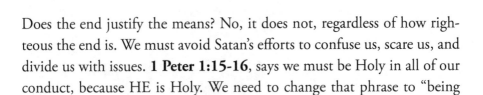

May 29

Does the end justify the means? No, it does not, regardless of how righteous the end is. We must avoid Satan's efforts to confuse us, scare us, and divide us with issues. **1 Peter 1:15-16**, says we must be Holy in all of our conduct, because HE is Holy. We need to change that phrase to "being Holy is always justified, regardless of the ends."

✝

Key Bible Verse

1 Peter 1:15-16 – "But just as he who called you is holy, so be holy in all you do; for it is written: "Be holy, because I am holy."

Prayers & Notes

_____

_____

_____

_____

_____

_____

_____

_____

A Blessing from Yesterday _____

Something I am Thankful for Today _____

Patrick E. Moore

May 30

Remember the old flash bulbs for cameras? Wow, they were hot to handle and would temporarily blind you when they went off. This morning, I noticed the sunlight bouncing off the waves at the lake, and it reminded me of those old flashbulbs. The Apostle Paul must have been blinded by what seemed like a thousand lightbulbs, and it changed his life. **Acts 22.6.** May the flash of GOD's brilliance change your life today.

†

Key Bible Verse

Acts 22.6 - "About noon as I came near Damascus, suddenly a bright light from heaven flashed around me."

Prayers & Notes

_____

_____

_____

_____

_____

_____

_____

A Blessing from Yesterday _____

Something I am Thankful for Today _____

May 31

An underlying feature is not easily recognized because it's not obvious. Underlying currents in the air and water are dangerous for pilots, boaters and swimmers. The most dangerous, however, are the underlying sins of prejudice, bias, greed and pride, even for Christians. They can cause division and destroy a society. Pray for GOD's intervention and influence in and on our lives today!

Key Bible Verse

James 2:1 – "My brothers and sisters, believers in our glorious Lord Jesus Christ must not show favoritism."

Prayers & Notes

_____

_____

_____

_____

_____

_____

A Blessing from Yesterday _____

Something I am Thankful for Today _____

June 1

It was still dark when I went out this morning, and our gas lamp's flickering flame was lighting the sidewalk like it has continually for the last twenty-five years. It reminded me that lamps had a significant role in the Bible in verses like **Psalms 119:105,** "Your WORD is a lamp to my feet and a light to my path." May GOD's lamp of righteousness light your way today.

Key Bible Verse

Psalms 119:105 – "Your word is a lamp for my feet, a light on my path."

Prayers & Notes

_____

_____

_____

_____

_____

_____

_____

A Blessing from Yesterday _____

Something I am Thankful for Today _____

June 2

While sitting on a dock last weekend watching my grandkids fish, I started thinking about the famous song "The Dock of the Bay" by Otis Redding. Did you know Otis died at age 26 two days after recording his famous song? Then, I thought about JESUS who probably sat on a dock watching some guys fish, guys HE would later ask to follow HIM so they could become fishers of men. **Matthew 4:19**. Join me and follow HIM today, ok?

✝

Key Bible Verse

Matthew 4:19 - "Come, follow me," Jesus said, "and I will send you out to fish for people."

Prayers & Notes

_____

_____

_____

_____

_____

_____

_____

A Blessing from Yesterday _____

Something I am Thankful for Today _____

Patrick E. Moore

June 3

Remember, there is no ocean that can't be parted, no mountain that can't be moved, no heart that can't be softened, no mind that GOD can't be change and no person that GOD can't reach. We just have to have faith. **Hebrews 11:1** says, "faith is the assurance of things hoped for, the conviction of things not seen." Worship HIM today!

Key Bible Verse

Hebrews 11:1 – "Now faith is confidence in what we hope for and assurance about what we do not see."

Prayers & Notes

_____

_____

_____

_____

_____

_____

A Blessing from Yesterday _____

Something I am Thankful for Today _____

June 4

My model train layout will be a small town from the 1950's with ordinary people, one grocer, one doctor, a sheriff, a drug store, a drive-in theatre, a church...get the picture? Bethlehem was a small town of ordinary people but also the birthplace of David and later JESUS (**Micah 5:2**) who sought out the ordinary to bring Glory to HIS name. Feeling ordinary? Maybe GOD has great things in store for you today. Seek HIM!

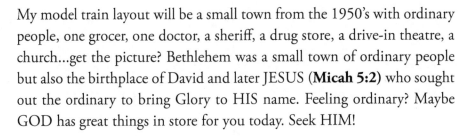

Key Bible Verse

Micah 5:2 - "But you, Bethlehem Ephrathah, though you are small among the clans of Judah, out of you will come for me one who will be ruler over Israel, whose origins are from of old from ancient times."

Prayers & Notes

_____

_____

_____

_____

_____

_____

_____

A Blessing from Yesterday _____

Something I am Thankful for Today _____

Patrick E. Moore

June 5

I first learned how to read a compass as a teen in the Boy Scouts. A compass works by always pointing to true north, so then you can orient yourself to where you are and where you want to go. Do you ever think about your moral compass? It's GOD's WORD. **Isaiah 58:11**. True north is the Spiritual direction towards GOD that we should travel. Sometimes we get off course, but GOD's WORD will always put us back on track. It never fails.

✝

Key Bible Verse

Isaiah 58:11 – "The LORD will guide you always; he will satisfy your needs in a sun-scorched land and will strengthen your frame. You will be like a well-watered garden, like a spring whose waters never fail."

Prayers & Notes

_____

_____

_____

_____

_____

_____

_____

A Blessing from Yesterday _____

Something I am Thankful for Today _____

June 6

Have you ever heard of a "breath prayer?" Starting in the 6th century, they were short prayers prayed with the rhythm of each breath. We celebrate the first breath and mourn the last one, but the question is what do you with the other 23,000 each day? Each breath we take is a blessing and gift from GOD, right? That's why I thank GOD each morning for another day of breath with HIS Grace. Don't take it for granted. **Psalms 23:3**.

Key Bible Verse

Psalms 23:3 – "he refreshes my soul. He guides me along the right paths for his name's sake."

Prayers & Notes

_____

_____

_____

_____

_____

_____

A Blessing from Yesterday _____

Something I am Thankful for Today _____

Patrick E. Moore

June 7

Emotions are natural. Our emotional makeup may differ, but we all have instances when our emotions seem to get out of control, especially anger, guilt and sadness. I know that JESUS expressed those same emotions, so what is the difference? The difference is that JESUS never used them for selfish needs or desires. Let's treat each other with kindness. **Colossians 3:12-14**

Key Bible Verse

Colossians 3:12 – "Therefore, as God's chosen people, holy and dearly loved, clothe yourselves with compassion, kindness, humility, gentleness and patience."

Prayers & Notes

_____

_____

_____

_____

_____

_____

_____

A Blessing from Yesterday _____

Something I am Thankful for Today _____

June 8

The words "hand" and "hands" are used in the Bible 1466 and 462 times respectively. Amazing, huh? Our hands can hold onto things good or bad. The same can be said for our lives. Sometimes GOD wants to put something into our hands to bless us or others, but we are holding on so tight to the wrong things, we won't let HIM. Relax your grip on the old things of life, and let GOD place HIS renewed Spirit in your hands. Let HIS Blessings flow. **Jeremiah 29:11.** Have a great day,

✝

Key Bible Verse

Jeremiah 29:11 – "For I know the plans I have for you," Declares the LORD, "plans to prosper you and not to harm you, plans to give you hope and a future."

Prayers & Notes

_____

_____

_____

_____

_____

_____

A Blessing from Yesterday _____

Something I am Thankful for Today _____

June 9

Today, I think becoming deaf would be harder than becoming blind. It's because I love the sounds of nature, music, the laugh of a child, words of encouragement and hearing GOD's WORD. The Bible speaks of spiritual deafness, a condition of not listening for GOD's voice and direction in our lives. In **Mark 7:32-34**, JESUS healed a deaf man, and that parable applies to us as well. Listen for HIS voice today. HE is calling.

Key Bible Verse

Mark 7:32-34 – "There some people brought to him a man who was deaf and could hardly talk, and they begged Jesus to place his hand on him. After he took him aside, away from the crowd, Jesus put his fingers into the man's ears. Then he spit and touched the man's tongue. He looked up to heaven and with a deep sigh said to him, *"Ephphatha!"* (which means "Be opened!")."

Prayers & Notes

_____

_____

_____

_____

_____

A Blessing from Yesterday _____

Something I am Thankful for Today _____

June 10

Did you know the car restoration business is almost a two billion dollar industry? I sure didn't. Restoration is the process of renewing, reviving or restoring something to its original and unimpaired condition. With all the turmoil in the world, my prayer is GOD will restore our hearts to HIS original design, before we were impaired by sin. Pray for a revival today. **Ezekiel 36:26**.

Key Bible Verse

Ezekiel 36:26 – "I will give you a new heart and put a new spirit in you; I will remove from you your heart of stone and give you a heart of flesh."

Prayers & Notes

_____

_____

_____

_____

_____

_____

_____

A Blessing from Yesterday _____

Something I am Thankful for Today _____

June 11

Studies show we make, on average, 35,000 Decisions each day. Wow! Some are big, most are little, but they all have consequences. Some turn out good and some not so good. How do we know if we are making the right decision each time? GOD's WORD is where we need to turn for the answers. **Proverbs 3:5-6** says, "Trust in the LORD with all your heart... and HE will make your paths straight." But to trust someone, you need to know HIM. Seek HIM!

Key Bible Verse

Proverbs 3:5-6 – "Trust in the LORD with all your heart and lean not on your own understanding; in all your ways submit to him, and he will make your paths straight "

Prayers & Notes

_____

_____

_____

_____

_____

_____

A Blessing from Yesterday _____

Something I am Thankful for Today _____

June 12

This morning, I hear a chain saw, a ladder going up and down, a chipper truck, birds singing...lots of noise. It reminds me that Satan always wants to distract us with noise in life to keep us from praying and worshipping our Heavenly Father. Do not let the distractions conform you to the world; be purposeful, focused, active, and find a time to be still. Most of all, keep your mind ON JESUS. **Romans 12:2**

Key Bible Verse

Romans 12:2 – "Do not conform to the pattern of this world but be transformed by the renewing of your mind. Then you will be able to test and approve what God's will is—his good, pleasing and perfect will."

Prayers & Notes

_____

_____

_____

_____

_____

_____

_____

A Blessing from Yesterday _____

Something I am Thankful for Today _____

Patrick E. Moore

June 13

We have a couple of large flowerpots that became brittle over time and broke. Instead of discarding them, my wife created new, beautiful arrangements with the broken parts. It reminds me that we are all broken in some way, but GOD can turn our brokenness into something beautiful, if we let HIM. **Ephesians 2:10**. Remember, GOD won't let a masterpiece go to waste, and we are all HIS masterpieces. GOD never gives up on us.

Key Bible Verse

Ephesians 2:10 – "For we are God's handiwork, created in Christ Jesus to do good works, which God prepared in advance for us to do."

Prayers & Notes

_____

_____

_____

_____

_____

_____

_____

A Blessing from Yesterday _____

Something I am Thankful for Today _____

June 14

The first traffic light was installed in Cleveland, Ohio, in 1914, and it replaced thousands of traffic cops. The average red light lasts seventy-five seconds, and an American living in a city will spend sixty hours each year waiting at a light. Here's an idea. The LORD's Prayer, (**Matthew 6:9-13**) only takes about twenty-five seconds to recite, so every time you sit at a red light, lift that prayer to your Heavenly FATHER. HE will bless you. Try it!

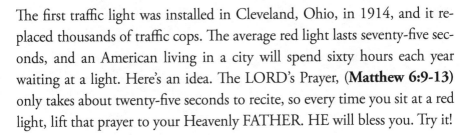

Key Bible Verse

Matthew 6:9-13 - "This, then, is how you should pray: "'Our Father in heaven, hallowed be your name, your kingdom come, your will be done, on earth as it is in heaven. Give us today our daily bread. And forgive us our debts, as we also have forgiven our debtors. And lead us not into temptation but deliver us from the evil one.'"

Prayers & Notes

_____

_____

_____

_____

_____

_____

A Blessing from Yesterday _____

Something I am Thankful for Today _____

June 15

If you write a book, you need a good editor who is detailed enough to look at your draft word by word and line by line. We are called to do something similar in reading scripture if we are to gain knowledge. **Isaiah 28:10** says to study "precept upon precept, line upon line, here a little, there a little" if you want to learn what GOD is trying to say to you. Let GOD's WORD be your guide today in this troubled world!

✝

Key Bible Verse

Isaiah 28:10 – "For it is: Do this, do that, a rule for this, a rule for that a little here, a little there."

Prayers & Notes

_____

_____

_____

_____

_____

_____

_____

_____

A Blessing from Yesterday _____

Something I am Thankful for Today _____

June 16

I like to tinker with tools, build and fix things in my SHOP. Sometimes, I modify a tool so it can perform another purpose. You know, sometimes GOD modifies our circumstances or helps us change our desires so we can accomplish another purpose...HIS Purpose. After all, HE is the Creator of all things. Is GOD working in your life right now? **2 Corinthians 5:17** confirms we become a new creation when we know HIM.

Key Bible Verse

2 Corinthians 5:17 – "Therefore, if anyone is in Christ, the new creation has come: The old has gone, the new is here!"

Prayers & Notes

_____

_____

_____

_____

_____

_____

A Blessing from Yesterday _____

Something I am Thankful for Today _____

Patrick E. Moore

June 17

Sometimes, people just push our buttons and bring out the worst in us. Can I have an Amen? Ok, we are humans who have emotions as did JESUS who seemed to lose HIS temper a time or two. But maybe, just maybe, we need to ask GOD to remove some of those buttons we have and help us deal with the worst inside our hearts. GOD's WORD has a lot to say about our temper. Check out **James 1:19-20.**

Key Bible Verse

James 1:19-20 – "My dear brothers and sisters, take note of this: Everyone should be quick to listen, slow to speak and slow to become angry, because human anger does not produce the righteousness that God desires."

Prayers & Notes

_____

_____

_____

_____

_____

_____

_____

A Blessing from Yesterday _____

Something I am Thankful for Today _____

June 18

Ever heard the idiom "in a pickle?" Let me clarify. A pickle, in baseball terms, is when a runner is caught between bases and is running to avoid the tag. A pickle, in life, could mean you're in some type of trouble or jam. I am speaking of the latter. Since we live in an imperfect world of choices and consequences, trouble is inevitable. Fear not. Stay close to GOD's WORD to get out of the pickles in life. **John 14:27**

✝

Key Bible Verse

John 14:27 – "Peace I leave with you; my peace I give you. I do not give to you as the world gives. Do not let your hearts be troubled and do not be afraid."

Prayers & Notes

_____

_____

_____

_____

_____

_____

_____

A Blessing from Yesterday _____

Something I am Thankful for Today _____

Patrick E. Moore

June 19

Our earthly journey is fragile and can be gone in an instant, right? The important thing is not how long our journey will be but what will be our final destination. With GOD's Grace, we are given a choice to make our destination Heaven, GOD's Home of eternal peace. Make sure you and your loved ones know JESUS, so they join you for eternity in paradise. **Luke 23:43**. Seek HIM!

Key Bible Verse

Luke 23:43 – "Jesus answered him, "Truly I tell you, today you will be with me in paradise

Prayers & Notes

_____

_____

_____

_____

_____

_____

A Blessing from Yesterday _____

Something I am Thankful for Today _____

June 20

I have been wiring the track on my train table to the power source (transformer) so my trains will operate without problems or possible derailments. That reminds me that we are connected to GOD's power by Grace and Faith. GOD's WORD is the spiritual wire that connects us. HIS power transforms us into a life of righteousness, so we won't derail off the tracks. **2 Corinthians 13:4**. Check your connections to GOD's Power today!

Key Bible Verse

2 Corinthians 13:4 – "For to be sure, he was crucified in weakness, yet he lives by God's power. Likewise, we are weak in him, yet by God's power we will live with him in our dealing with you."

Prayers & Notes

_____

_____

_____

_____

_____

_____

_____

A Blessing from Yesterday _____

Something I am Thankful for Today _____

Patrick E. Moore

June 21

"Keep me in the Moment" is the name of a Christian song about staying in the presence of GOD. The second part of the chorus says, "cause I don't wanna miss what you have for me." What an awesome message. GOD gives us blessings abundantly (**Ephesians 3:20-22**) but with prayer, worship, supplication and service to others, HIS Blessings will multiply. Let's not miss them; there are more to come. Praise HIM!

✝

Key Bible Verse

Ephesians 3:20-22 – "Now to him who is able to do immeasurably more than all we ask or imagine, according to his power that is at work within us, to him be glory in the church and in Christ Jesus throughout all generations, for ever and ever! Amen."

Prayers & Notes

_____

_____

_____

_____

_____

_____

A Blessing from Yesterday _____

Something I am Thankful for Today _____

June 22

Silk is one of the four main animal fibers along with wool, angora and camel hair. It's made from the cocoon fibers of the silkworm. It was discovered in China in the 1st century. There is no substitute for silk, only imitations. The same is true for our Creator who sent HIS son JESUS to die for our sins. There are no substitutes for JESUS and our eternal salvation, only imitations. **Ephesians 2:8-9**. Praise HIM!

Key Bible Verse

Ephesians 2:8-9 – "For it is by grace you have been saved, through faith—and this is not from yourselves, it is the gift of God – not by works, so that no one can boast."

Prayers & Notes

_____

_____

_____

_____

_____

_____

_____

A Blessing from Yesterday _____

Something I am Thankful for Today _____

Patrick E. Moore

June 23

Why do we become afraid which leads us to worry? Have you considered that being afraid and being discouraged are related? After all, the opposite of discouraged is encouraged (with courage). Why can we be encouraged if we know CHRIST? Because "HE who is in us is greater than he who is in the world" (**1 John 4:4**). "Do not be afraid" is a command from GOD. Let's trust and obey HIM today!

✝

Key Bible Verse

1 John 4:4 – "You, dear children, are from God and have overcome them, because the one who is in you is greater than the one who is in the world."

Prayers & Notes

_____

_____

_____

_____

_____

_____

A Blessing from Yesterday _____

Something I am Thankful for Today _____

June 24

It's been hot and dry recently, and our yard became parched. We turned on the water sprinklers for relief. As I look at the news, I see a world that is spiritually dry and parched from the heat of evil all around. We need to pray that GOD will turn on HIS Living Water sprinkler to bring relief to a dying world. Let's do our part. Sprinkle some of GODS living water on those around you today. **Isaiah 44:3**.

✝

Key Bible Verse

Isaiah 44:3 – "For I will pour water on the thirsty land, and streams on the dry ground; I will pour out my Spirit on your offspring, and my blessing on your descendants."

Prayers & Notes

_____

_____

_____

_____

_____

_____

_____

A Blessing from Yesterday _____

Something I am Thankful for Today _____

Patrick E. Moore

June 25

In pilot training, we practiced airplane spins so we could learn to get out of this dangerous spiral. The right choice was to look at the horizon and let go off the controls. That is applicable to life too when things begin to spiral out of control. We can choose defeat by hanging on to the struggle or look to GOD and let go & pray with a thankful heart. Don't forget we have choices. **Colossians 3:15**. Be Thankful.

Key Bible Verse

Colossians 3:15 – "Let the peace of Christ rule in your hearts, since as members of one body you were called to peace. And be thankful."

Prayers & Notes

_____

_____

_____

_____

_____

_____

_____

A Blessing from Yesterday _____

Something I am Thankful for Today _____

June 26

One of my favorite songs from 1969 was "More Today than Yesterday" by Spiral Staircase. It's a great pop tune about loving someone more today than yesterday. Thank goodness that's not how GOD loves us. GOD will not love our future selves more than our present selves. Yep, He also loved us the same yesterday, and "we love because HE first loved us" (**1 John 4:19**). Nothing we do will change that. Wow! Thank HIM

Key Bible Verse

1 John 4:19 – "We love because he first loved us."

Prayers & Notes

_____

_____

_____

_____

_____

_____

_____

A Blessing from Yesterday _____

Something I am Thankful for Today _____

Patrick E. Moore

June 27

The days seem to go by so much quicker as I get older, and the list of things I want to do just gets longer. Go figure. Here is a tip for everyone: make each moment count. You see, moments pass by and then they're gone. Fill your moments and days with hope, joy and love that can come only from knowing CHRIST JESUS, and you will be renewed each day. **2 Corinthians 4:15-16**. Thank HIM for today!

Key Bible Verse

2 Corinthians 4:15-16. – "All this is for your benefit, so that the grace that is reaching more and more people may cause thanksgiving to overflow to the glory of God. Therefore we do not lose heart. Though outwardly we are wasting away, yet inwardly we are being renewed day by day."

Prayers & Notes

_____

_____

_____

_____

_____

_____

A Blessing from Yesterday _____

Something I am Thankful for Today _____

June 28

"Going against the grain" is an idiom made famous by Shakespeare. The context was doing something opposite from your normal routine such as traveling a road less travelled. It also applies to Christians. JESUS lived HIS entire life on Earth against the grain. He teaches us to look to the Kingdom of GOD and not to the kingdom of man (**John 5:30**). Don't be fooled into living the way the world is going. Start living against the grain.

✝

Key Bible Verse

John 5:30 – "By myself I can do nothing; I judge only as I hear, and my judgment is just, for I seek not to please myself but him who sent me"

Prayers & Notes

_____

_____

_____

_____

_____

_____

_____

A Blessing from Yesterday _____

Something I am Thankful for Today _____

Patrick E. Moore

June 29

Sometimes we tease about people who think they "know it all." We can agree that is not a complimentary description of a person. But there is a "know it all" written about in the Bible, and it is our Heavenly FATHER. He also sees it all, so there is no hiding our deeds, thoughts and actions from HIM. **Proverbs 5:21.** Seek holiness in everything you do and remember GOD's watching.

Key Bible Verse

Proverbs 5:21 – "For your ways are in full view of the LORD, and he examines all your paths."

Prayers & Notes

_____

_____

_____

_____

_____

_____

_____

A Blessing from Yesterday _____

Something I am Thankful for Today _____

June 30

Monet, a radical French painter in the 1800's, was the father of impressionist art which features nature, bold colors the illusion of intense light. Monet said he wanted "to rescue art from the camera." It's interesting that GOD, the Creator of nature and light, sent HIS Son JESUS to earth with a radical message of love and grace and to become the light to rescue man from his sinful self. What a beautiful portrait that is. **John 3:21.**

Key Bible Verse

John 3:21 – "But whoever lives by the truth comes into the light, so that it may be seen plainly that what they have done has been done in the sight of God."

Prayers & Notes

_____

_____

_____

_____

_____

_____

_____

A Blessing from Yesterday _____

Something I am Thankful for Today _____

182   Patrick E. Moore

July 1

It's a rainy morning offering cool relief from the hot, dusty days we have had recently. GOD pours down the rain to a thirsty land just like HE pours down HIS Righteousness when we're feeling needy. GOD's people received such a pouring out of righteousness after their return from Babylon (**Isaiah 45:18**). As you enjoy the rain thank GOD for pouring out HIS Love on us each day. Be thankful, and don't take for granted GOD's Grace. Amen

Key Bible Verse

Isaiah 45:18 – "For this is what the LORD says— he who created the heavens, he is God; he who fashioned and made the earth, he founded it; he did not create it to be empty but formed it to be inhabited— he says: "I am the LORD, and there is no other."

Prayers & Notes

_____

_____

_____

_____

_____

_____

A Blessing from Yesterday _____

Something I am Thankful for Today _____

July 2

There's a warning on most side windows of cars that "objects are closer than they appear." The mirror's concave shape makes objects smaller and tricks our brains. Often, Satan, tries to trick our brains by making obstacles, worries and concerns seem bigger than they are. Remember, GOD will not give us more than we can handle (**1 Corinthians 10:13**). Trust HIM! GOD is bigger than any problem you could have.

Key Bible Verse

1 Corinthians 10:13 – "No temptation has overtaken you except what is common to mankind. And God is faithful; he will not let you be tempted beyond what you can bear. But when you are tempted, he will also provide a way out so that you can endure it."

Prayers & Notes

_____

_____

_____

_____

_____

A Blessing from Yesterday _____

Something I am Thankful for Today _____

Patrick E. Moore

July 3

The Ark of the Covenant was carried by the Israelites for 40 years in the desert. It carried a bowl with manna, the staff of Aaron and the Ten Commandments. It reminded the people that GOD provides, protects and guides. It disappeared after the Babylonians destroyed the temple. For us, JESUS is our provider and protector today and every day. **Philippians 4:19**. We carry HIM in our heart. HE's always there! Praise HIM!

Key Bible Verse

Philippians 4:19 – "And my God will meet all your needs according to the riches of his glory in Christ Jesus."

Prayers & Notes

_____

_____

_____

_____

_____

_____

A Blessing from Yesterday _____

Something I am Thankful for Today _____

July 4

I awoke this morning with the daylight seeping in through the closed, wooden shutters. It reminded me that GOD's light shines each day to break the darkness of the night. It's one of HIS creation promises. Since the fall of man, people have tried to shut out or block the light of GOD from shining. **John 1:5** gives us the promise of GOD's light in us and in the world. His light will shine and darkness will not win. Praise HIM!

✝

Key Bible Verse

John 1:5 – "The light shines in the darkness, and the darkness has not overcome it."

Prayers & Notes

_____

_____

_____

_____

_____

_____

A Blessing from Yesterday _____

Something I am Thankful for Today _____

July 5

I went to bed thinking about freedom as we closed out another July 4th celebration. I have learned that with freedom comes responsibility, or it can be taken away. As a CHRIST follower, we have the ultimate freedom. That is the freedom from sin and condemnation and a promise to be with HIM for eternity. **2 Corinthians 3:17**. Our only responsibility is to love everyone like CHRIST loved us. Let's celebrate that daily!

Key Bible Verse

2 Corinthians 3:17 – "Now the Lord is the Spirit, and where the Spirit of the Lord is, there is freedom."

Prayers & Notes

_____

_____

_____

_____

_____

_____

_____

A Blessing from Yesterday _____

Something I am Thankful for Today _____

July 6

I don't have a garden like our kids do, but I do know that seeds need good soil to be able to grow. That thought came from our sermon this morning about JESUS and the parable of the seed in Mark, chapter 4. Good soil and good seed will produce good fruit. Our heart is the soil and GOD's WORD is the seed of Truth. Please be aware that we can't change our own soil (heart), but GOD can. **Ezekiel 36:26**. Trust HIM!

Key Bible Verse

Ezekiel 36:26 – "I will give you a new heart and put a new spirit in you; I will remove from you your heart of stone and give you a heart of flesh."

Prayers & Notes

_____

_____

_____

_____

_____

_____

A Blessing from Yesterday _____

Something I am Thankful for Today _____

Patrick E. Moore

July 7

The WORD GOD awoke me with this morning was "plan." A simple definition is "an intention or decision to do something." You might say it is a desire for the direction to go. Guess what? Plans change, don't they? Maybe we didn't include GOD in our plans in the first place, or maybe they don't coincide with the plan GOD has in store for us. **Jeremiah 29:11**. Stop, pray, and listen for GOD's direction. HE will give you the right plan!

✝

Key Bible Verse

Jeremiah 29:11 – "For I know the plans I have for you," Declares the LORD, "plans to prosper you and not to harm you, plans to give you hope and a future."

Prayers & Notes

_____

_____

_____

_____

_____

_____

_____

A Blessing from Yesterday _____

Something I am Thankful for Today _____

July 8

My grandson's baseball team rallied from 7 runs down in the last inning to win against a really good team. Don't you love a good comeback? You know, the Bible is full of comeback stories – Moses, David, Daniel and friends, Ruth, Esther, Joshua, and more. But the story of JESUS is my favorite story. He was beaten, tortured, nailed to a cross and killed, but He made HIS comeback from the grave. He died for our sins to win against evil once and for all for those who believe. Now that's a comeback story! **John 11:25-26.** Worship HIM today.

Key Bible Verse

John 11:25-26 – "Jesus said to her, "I am the resurrection and the life. The one who believes in me will live, even though they die; and whoever lives by believing in me will never die. Do you believe this?"

Prayers & Notes

_____

_____

_____

_____

_____

A Blessing from Yesterday _____

Something I am Thankful for Today _____

Patrick E. Moore

July 9

We love our Koi fishpond and waterfall in the backyard, but the water has become icky, murky and not clear. We need to do a deep clean on it. You know, sometimes life gets the same way, especially the "not clear" part. Even though life is great, and we might be blessed beyond our imaginations, the future about some things might seem murky and troubling. **Proverbs 3:5-6** is a great passage to turn to. GOD's WORD always seems to clear things up. Amen

✝

Key Bible Verse

Proverbs 3:5-6 – "Trust in the LORD with all your heart and lean not on your own understanding; in all your ways submit to him, and he will make your paths straight"

Prayers & Notes

_____

_____

_____

_____

_____

_____

A Blessing from Yesterday _____

Something I am Thankful for Today _____

July 10

Unfortunately, there seems to be a lot of unhappy people in the world. It makes me wonder if they have broken hearts from disappointment or crushed spirits from their experiences. Either way, GOD can fix those things and help you fulfill the purpose HE has in store for your life. Try reading **Psalms 34:18,** and allow GOD to begin the healing process. Thank HIM!

Key Bible Verse

Psalms 34:18 – "The LORD is close to the brokenhearted and saves those who are crushed in spirit."

Prayers & Notes

_____

_____

_____

_____

_____

_____

A Blessing from Yesterday _____

Something I am Thankful for Today _____

Patrick E. Moore

July 11

Don't you sometimes wish that we had a news channel or radio station that reports only good news? What might that look like? Maybe you would listen in the morning and have hope for a blessed rest of the day, or maybe you would listen in the evening and go to bed happy and thankful. I am happy to report that GOD's WORD is the good news you are looking for. **Mark 1:15**. I think it's time to turn off the bad news and open up the GOOD NEWS!

Key Bible Verse

Mark 1:15 - "The time has come," he said. "The kingdom of God has come near. Repent and believe the good news!"

Prayers & Notes

_____

_____

_____

_____

_____

_____

_____

A Blessing from Yesterday _____

Something I am Thankful for Today _____

July 12

Do you carry some emergency items in your car in case of car trouble? I do. I have jumper cables, a flashlight, rope, small tool kit, first-aid kit, etc. Being prepared is a good motto. So, what do you carry for personal trouble such as anger, depression, anxiety, pride overload and sin in general? That's easy; carry a Bible. It is the instruction manual for all of our troubles. **Psalms 46:1**. Keep it close to you.

Key Bible Verse

Psalms 46:1 – "God is our refuge and strength, an ever-present help in trouble."

Prayers & Notes

_____

_____

_____

_____

_____

_____

A Blessing from Yesterday _____

Something I am Thankful for Today _____

July 13

One of my favorite hymns is starts, "Softly and tenderly JESUS is calling..." The words of the refrain, "come home, come home," remind me of happy times as a boy when Mom would say those words. No doubt about it, I am a home body. And if we like home now, wait until we get to Heaven. The Bible says it will be paradise (**Luke 23:43**). Therefore, even if you live in an earthly place of disappointment and discontent, if "you know that you know" JESUS, rejoice in knowing that one day He will call us home.

Key Bible Verse

Luke 23:43 – "Jesus answered him, "Truly I tell you, today you will be with me in paradise."

Prayers & Notes

_____

_____

_____

_____

_____

_____

A Blessing from Yesterday _____

Something I am Thankful for Today _____

July 14

Last night after dinner, as I began closing the blinds on a setting sun, I started humming the tune to the old Elton John song, "Don't Let the Sun Go Down on Me." Remember it? It was a long song about losing a relationship. Thank goodness our relationship with GOD is not like that if we stay close to HIM. The Bible says in **Ecclesiastes 1:5** that the sun will go up and down, but the light of GOD's righteousness never dims. Thank HIM today for HIS eternal light in your life.

✝

Key Bible Verse

Ecclesiastes 1:5 - "The sun rises and the sun sets, and hurries back to where it rises"

Prayers & Notes

_____

_____

_____

_____

_____

_____

_____

A Blessing from Yesterday _____

Something I am Thankful for Today _____

Patrick E. Moore

July 15

While walking to my car late yesterday afternoon, I noticed my shadow on the pavement ahead of me. I watched it lead me to the car. Then I remembered its GOD's shadow I am walking in, and because of that, I have nothing to fear. **Isaiah 51:16** says GOD covers us with the shadow of HIS hand, and because of HIS eternal light, the shadow of GOD's hand will never leave us. Find comfort today in HIM. Every time you see your shadow, remember GOD is with you.

Key Bible Verse

Isaiah 51:16 – "I have put my words in your mouth and covered you with the shadow of my hand— I who set the heavens in place, who laid the foundations of the earth, and who say to Zion, 'You are my people.'"

Prayers & Notes

_____

_____

_____

_____

_____

_____

A Blessing from Yesterday _____

Something I am Thankful for Today _____

July 16

Healing comes in many forms. I certainly have experienced GOD's healing hand in my physical life, but our hearts and souls need healing, too. I got some heart healing last night watching a blind and severely autistic boy named Kodi stun the audience and judges on the show "America's Got Talent." You see, when he plays the piano and sings, you would never know he has any problems. Amazing. His mother said music saved his life, and now he encourages others with his talent. GOD has given us all gifts, talents and a purpose to serve and honor HIM and others. Embrace what you have and who you are. GOD CAN USE YOU.

✝

Key Bible Verse

Romans 12:6 – "We have different gifts, according to the grace given to each of us."

Prayers & Notes

_____

_____

_____

_____

_____

A Blessing from Yesterday _____

Something I am Thankful for Today _____

July 17

The word "obey" in our Bible is a translation of the Jewish word "shema," meaning "to hear." JESUS gave us many commands in the New Testament, not suggestions. The greatest command is found in **Matthew 22:37-39** which says you should love the LORD OUR GOD with "all your heart." The second is to love your neighbor. Wouldn't you agree it's hard to obey a command if you don't hear it in the first place? Therefore, take some time each day to hear the WORD of GOD, and then do your best to obey. You will be blessed.

Key Bible Verse

Matthew 22:37-38 –"Jesus replied: "'Love the Lord your God with all your heart and with all your soul and with all your mind. This is the first and greatest commandment"

Prayers & Notes

_____

_____

_____

_____

_____

_____

A Blessing from Yesterday _____

Something I am Thankful for Today _____

July 18

This morning, I noticed a few nails on the back deck floor sticking up that need to be driven down. Immediately, my mind went to the nails that were driven into JESUS on a cross over 2000 years ago. The nails used by Romans for crucifixions were made of 7 to 9-inch lengths of iron and were driven into the wrists and feet to keep the body in place and in excruciating pain until the person died, usually of suffocation. Be the way, did you know the word "excruciating" in Latin means "to crucify?" Remember JESUS when you hear or read that word. What a Savior! HE came to die for the sins of the world. **1 Corinthians 15:3**. Let this day be one of remembrance and thanksgiving. Today, let us praise the one who died for you and me. Amen.

Key Bible Verse

1 Corinthians 15:3 – "For what I received I passed on to you as of first importance: that Christ died for our sins according to the Scriptures,"

Prayers & Notes

_____

_____

_____

_____

_____

A Blessing from Yesterday _____

Something I am Thankful for Today _____

Patrick E. Moore

July 19

"Looking for a few good men" has been an effective recruiting slogan for the Marines since 1779 – wow, over 200 years. Speaking of fighters, what do you think GOD is looking for in us to help fight the spiritual battle of good and evil? **Ephesians 6:12**. Ideally, HE would want us to have the Faith of Daniel and the Hope of Moses and the heart of KING David. By the way, GOD will give us these qualities if we seek them earnestly. With those qualities and GOD's WORD, which is the sword of Truth, we become GOD's Heavenly Realm Marines in hopes of winning more souls for CHRIST. Ooh rah!

Key Bible Verse

Ephesians 6:12 – "For our struggle is not against flesh and blood, but against the rulers, against the authorities, against the powers of this dark world and against the spiritual forces of evil in the heavenly realms."

Prayers & Notes

_____

_____

_____

_____

_____

_____

A Blessing from Yesterday _____

Something I am Thankful for Today _____

July 20

Do you believe in angels? I awoke thinking about them this morning. They are mentioned 263 times in the Bible. They are Spirit beings, faithful and obedient to GOD, sent to watch over and protect those who will inherit the Kingdom of GOD. **Hebrews 1:14**. I wonder how many times they have protected me and my loved ones from evil, sin and disaster. We need to thank GOD daily for the Angels HE has sent to protect us!

Key Bible Verse

Hebrews 1:14. – "Are they not all ministering spirits sent forth to minister for those who will inherit salvation?"

Prayers & Notes

_____

_____

_____

_____

_____

_____

_____

A Blessing from Yesterday _____

Something I am Thankful for Today _____

July 21

This morning, the word persecution comes to mind. The definition is "hostility and ill-treatment, especially because of race, political or religious beliefs." Christians have been persecuted around the world ever since JESUS walked the earth. What are we to do and how are we to act are the questions. First, we are called to be bold and unashamed of our Faith (**2 Timothy 2:14-16**). Understand persecution will not end on this side of Heaven, but GOD will honor those who are persecuted. **Matthew 5:10-12**. Stand bold in HIS WORD today!

Key Bible Verse

Matthew 5:10 - "Blessed are those who are persecuted because of righteousness, for theirs is the kingdom of heaven."

Prayers & Notes

_____

_____

_____

_____

_____

_____

A Blessing from Yesterday _____

Something I am Thankful for Today _____

July 22

It's been proven that being around water helps your emotional and mental state. A book written about this subject calls it our "blue mind" state, where peace and tranquility are more prevalent. Two days ago, while walking Meili, our 5-pound Shih Tzu, we stopped by the creek and just sat quietly. Even Meili joined me in the tranquility and laid down in the still water. **Psalms 23:2** talks about GOD leading us by the still water, and water is mentioned over 700 times in the Bible. May GOD's Living Water bring you peace today.

Key Bible Verse

Psalms 23:2 – "He makes me lie down in green pastures; he leads me beside quiet waters"

Prayers & Notes

_____

_____

_____

_____

_____

A Blessing from Yesterday _____

Something I am Thankful for Today _____

Patrick E. Moore

July 23

In the insurance or financial world, a covenant is an agreement between two parties that cover certain points. It is impossible to cover all contingencies with a single covenant. The Good News for Christians is that the new covenant that GOD has given us, brought about through the death and resurrection of JESUS CHRIST, does cover all sins and contingencies. It assures us of eternal life, regardless of when, where and how we might have broken our covenant with GOD through sinning. You can trust GOD to keep HIS WORD. THANK HIM today!

Key Bible Verse

1 Peter 2:24 - "He himself bore our sins" in his body on the cross, so that we might die to sins and live for righteousness; "by his wounds you have been healed."

Prayers & Notes

_____

_____

_____

_____

_____

_____

A Blessing from Yesterday _____

Something I am Thankful for Today _____

July 24

During a hot summer like we have been experiencing lately, all of nature is dry and thirsty for water. The last few days, we have had needed showers that bring the joy of rain to our trees, grass and flowers. That reminds me that during extended periods of uncertainty, our hearts and souls get dry and thirsty just like a hot summer. It may lead to anxiousness, worry, and lost hope. We need the joy of GOD's Living Water to fall on us to refresh us again. Let prayer and GOD's WORD cure the dryness. **Proverbs 25:25**

Key Bible Verse

Proverbs 25:25 – "Like cold water to a weary soul is good news from a distant land."

Prayers & Notes

_____

_____

_____

_____

_____

_____

A Blessing from Yesterday _____

Something I am Thankful for Today _____

Patrick E. Moore

July 25

I heard in a Christian song yesterday the lyric, "I am sick and tired of being sick and tired," and thought there are probably a lot of people who would agree with that statement today. Yes, we are living in limbo due to a worldwide virus, we're not sure when normal life will resume, and Satan is using this time to further attack our Christian Principles. But do not fear. As Christians, we have the Good News of a Savior who will never leave or forsake us. **Hebrews 13:5-6**. Trust HIM today.

Key Bible Verse

Hebrew 13:5-6 – "Keep your lives free from the love of money and be content with what you have, because God has said, "Never will I leave you; never will I forsake you." So we say with confidence, "The Lord is my helper; I will not be afraid. What can mere mortals do to me?"

Prayers & Notes

_____

_____

_____

_____

_____

A Blessing from Yesterday _____

Something I am Thankful for Today _____

July 26

Our daily lives are shaped by daily habits, some good and some bad. Agreed? Where do our habits come from, and how do they start? Our habits tell a lot about who we are. The Bible tells us in **Proverbs 27:19** our hearts are a reflection of who we really are. Speaking of the Bible, according to a recent survey, only 9% of Americans read the Bible daily while 34% say they never read it at all. Surprising? Probably not, but it speaks loudly to why our country is in a spiritual decline and increasing turmoil. For the last 585 days, I am proud to be in the 9% that read the Bible daily. Hopefully you will read the key verse in this daily devotion, and we can improve the results of the next survey.

Key Bible Verse

Proverbs 27:19 – "As water reflects the face, so one's life reflects the heart."

Prayers & Notes

_____

_____

_____

_____

_____

A Blessing from Yesterday _____

Something I am Thankful for Today _____

Patrick E. Moore

July 27

What does the phrase "being present" mean to you? To me, it means being in the moment, really focused on someone or something. Living in a world of distractions makes "being present" really hard, even with GOD. Would you agree? But it's really important and will require some new discipline! You see, our relationships with our parents, spouses, kids, grandkids and friends are everything, and if we are "not present," those relationships will suffer. The same is true with our relationship with GOD. We must find a way to "be present in our worship" and when we do, GOD will be present with us. **Psalms 46:10** says it well, "be still and know that I am GOD." Be still and be present with others today.

Key Bible Verse

Psalms 46:10 – "He says, "Be still, and know that I am God; I will be exalted among the nations, I will be exalted in the earth."

Prayers & Notes

_____

_____

_____

_____

_____

A Blessing from Yesterday _____

Something I am Thankful for Today _____

July 28

"Did you hear me?" and "Were you listening?" are probably questions we have asked or heard in the last week, right? The answer to the first question is always "yes," because hearing, the perceiving of sound, is automatic. However, it may have been heard as blah, blah, blah, because we weren't listening. Listening requires a relationship, concentration and ends with taking action. **James 1:22** says "don't merely listen to GOD's WORD but do what it says." Tune in to GOD's WORD today! HE may be calling you; are you listening?

Key Bible Verse

James 1:22 – "Do not merely listen to the word, and so deceive yourselves. Do what it says."

Prayers & Notes

_____

_____

_____

_____

_____

_____

A Blessing from Yesterday _____

Something I am Thankful for Today _____

Patrick E. Moore

July 29

The origin and history of candles goes back thousands of years, and they were first made with animal fat, then beeswax and now petroleum-based paraffin. They still provide light in places without electricity. Candlelight came from the ingenuity given to man by an omnipotent GOD, but candles will still burn out. This is not true for the light of GOD which will shine eternally. **Revelation 22:5** says that when we are in Heaven, there will be no need for candles or even the sun, because GOD's radiance will illuminate us forever. Let each candle you see remind you of GOD's eternal light.

Key Bible Verse

Revelation 22:5 – "There will be no more night. They will not need the light of a lamp or the light of the sun, for the Lord God will give them light. And they will reign for ever and ever."

Prayers & Notes

_____

_____

_____

_____

_____

_____

A Blessing from Yesterday _____

Something I am Thankful for Today _____

July 30

Yes, even people of GOD face giants in their life. Some obstacles seem too big to conquer or get past. Along with the giant usually comes a voice of doubt, fear or hopelessness. The same thing happened in the story of Goliath that unfolds in in **1 Samuel 17**. The voice of a single giant stopped the army of GOD. Really? After what GOD had done for them? You see, even when GOD has done miraculous things in our lives, giants keep appearing. Then, along comes an ordinary person, like you or me...his name was David. His faith statement is in 1 **Samuel 17:37**. Remember what GOD has done for you. HE can defeat any giant you and I might face. Have Faith today!

Key Bible Verse

I Samuel 17:37 – "The LORD who rescued me from the paw of the lion and the paw of the bear will rescue me from the hand of this Philistine. Saul said to David, Go, and the LORD be with you."

Prayers & Notes

_____

_____

_____

_____

_____

A Blessing from Yesterday _____

Something I am Thankful for Today _____

Patrick E. Moore

July 31

Let's talk reality, shall we? We live on planet Earth, technically a big rock, and some of us will die today and most won't. I am not talking about a virus but about the statistics of life. As a Believer in JESUS CHRIST, I say "so what?" HE is my Rock, and whether I live or die, I will be with HIM on earth or in Heaven. **1 Thessalonians 5:9-10**. How amazing is that thought? We are all sinners and certainly don't deserve CHRIST, but HE died for our sins to make that possible. Are you standing on the Rock of Salvation today? If not, step on and know you will be with HIM in life or death.

Key Bible Verse

1 Thessalonians 5:9-10 – "For God did not appoint us to suffer wrath but to receive salvation through our Lord Jesus Christ. He died for us so that, whether we are awake or asleep, we may live together with him."

Prayers & Notes

_____

_____

_____

_____

_____

A Blessing from Yesterday _____

Something I am Thankful for Today _____

August 1

Ever driven on a small mountain road on a foggy night? We did last night when driving to North Carolina after being detoured off the interstate. It was a white-knuckle experience, for sure. This morning, it reminds me detours in life are sometimes unavoidable, and the fog of life can limit your vision of where you are going. Stop, and turn to prayer and GOD's WORD. HE will clear the fog. **Hebrews 11:1** says, "now Faith is confidence in what we hope for and assurance of what we do not see." Praise HIM today.

✝

Key Bible Verse

Hebrews 11:1 – "Now faith is confidence in what we hope for and assurance about what we do not see."

Prayers & Notes

_____

_____

_____

_____

_____

_____

_____

A Blessing from Yesterday _____

Something I am Thankful for Today _____

Patrick E. Moore

August 2

"Hang on to what you got" is a line of a hit song by the Four Seasons in 1966 about hanging on to a girl in a marriage. It made me think we have a lot we need to hang on to during life, relationships, jobs, money, good habits etc. However, the most important thing to hang on to is Faith in JESUS CHRIST. **Proverbs 3:6** is a good verse to ponder when you are trying to decide what to hang on to and what to let go. Let GOD guide your steps today and tomorrow. HE will keep you on the right path!

Key Bible Verse

Proverbs 3:6 – "in all your ways submit to him, and he will make your paths straight."

Prayers & Notes

_____

_____

_____

_____

_____

_____

_____

A Blessing from Yesterday _____

Something I am Thankful for Today _____

August 3

Does your mind wander? Academia might say it is "task unrelated thought." Of course, we all have active thoughts, and they enter our minds constantly. Our thoughts can come from lots of sources, both good and bad. We must guard our minds especially from Satan. He wants us to believe his lies, because if we do, then he can lead us to sin. The Apostle Paul tells us in **Romans 12:2** not to be conformed to this world but to renew our minds daily in CHRIST. Keep HIM on your mind daily.

✝

Key Bible Verse

Romans 12:2 – "Do not conform to the pattern of this world but be transformed by the renewing of your mind. Then you will be able to test and approve what God's will is—his good, pleasing and perfect will."

Prayers & Notes

_____

_____

_____

_____

_____

_____

A Blessing from Yesterday _____

Something I am Thankful for Today _____

August 4

"Jehovah Jireh" means "the LORD will provide." This name for GOD is found in **Genesis 22:12-14** after GOD provided a ram to Abraham for a sacrifice instead of his son Isaac. Unfortunately, we are living in a selfish and secular world that is looking in all the wrong places for the things we want instead of what we need. Here is the truth: GOD will provide! With prayer and the reading of GOD's WORD, you find that JEHOVAH JIREH will provide everything you need. Thank HIM today with your praise.

Key Bible Verse

Genesis 22:13-14 – "Abraham looked up and there in a thicket he saw a ram caught by its horns. He went over and took the ram and sacrificed it as a burnt offering instead of his son. So Abraham called that place The LORD Will Provide. And to this day it is said, "On the mountain of the LORD it will be provided.""

Prayers & Notes

_____

_____

_____

_____

_____

A Blessing from Yesterday _____

Something I am Thankful for Today _____

No Mountain Too High   217

August 5

We watched one of our favorite movies yesterday. "Seabiscuit" is a true story about an undersized and underdog thoroughbred racing horse in 1938-1940. One of the best lines in the movie is delivered when the jockey, Red Pollard, answered reporters' questions about why his horse was so good. He said, "it's not in his feet but his heart." I love that line, and it reminds me of what GOD is looking for in us when HE calls us to HIM. HE is not looking for our physical ability, HE is looking for our heart availability. **Mark 12:30** says "love GOD with all your heart." Turn your heart to GOD today.

✝

Key Bible Verse

Mark 12:30 – "Love the Lord your God with all your heart and with all your soul and with all your mind and with all your strength."

Prayers & Notes

_____

_____

_____

_____

_____

_____

A Blessing from Yesterday _____

Something I am Thankful for Today _____

Patrick E. Moore

August 6

The journey of life is different for each of us, but you likely agree it is sometimes easy and sometimes difficult. Using a sailboat analogy, sometimes the wind is blowing, sometimes it's not. Sometimes you even may have to paddle. It's all part of GOD's plan for life. And maybe the journey is more about who we are becoming than where we are going. Embrace GOD's journey for your life. GOD has a plan for you and will give you hope for the future, **Jeremiah 29:11**.

Key Bible Verse

Jeremiah 29:11 – "For I know the plans I have for you," declares the Lord, "plans to prosper you and not to harm you, plans to give you hope and a future."

Prayers & Notes

A Blessing from Yesterday _____

Something I am Thankful for Today _____

August 7

Last night, I noticed the loud chorus of sound coming from the crickets, katydids, grasshoppers and cicadas in our wooded front yard. Based on statistics, I could have a million insects in my front yard alone. The male cicadas' clicks and chirps can be heard a mile away. Wow. No wonder it's loud. I love the sounds of summer that will be with us until the first frost. They are all part of GOD's perfect creation as stated in **Proverbs 16:4**. My prayer today is that we acknowledge and thank GOD for HIS Creation... even our loud, little insect buddies.

Key Bible Verse

Proverbs 16:4 – "The LORD works out everything to its proper end—even the wicked for a day of disaster."

Prayers & Notes

_____

_____

_____

_____

_____

_____

A Blessing from Yesterday _____

Something I am Thankful for Today _____

Patrick E. Moore

August 8

Did you know that over 44,000 corneal implants are done each year with probably ten times that number on a waiting list? My mother died in 1985 and was a cornea donor. It was so rewarding to receive a letter informing us someone, who had been blind could now see because of my Mom's eyes. What is worse than physical blindness? Spiritual blindness. When we become a follower of JESUS CHRIST, HE gives us a Spiritual Transplant so we can see through HIS eyes the things HE wants us to see. Trust HIM TODAY! **Mark. 8:25**

Key Bible Verse

Mark. 8:25 – "Once more Jesus put his hands on the man's eyes. Then his eyes were opened, his sight was restored, and he saw everything clearly."

Prayers & Notes

_____

_____

_____

_____

_____

_____

A Blessing from Yesterday _____

Something I am Thankful for Today _____

August 9

Today is "Reset Sunday" at our church, meaning we are going back to regularly scheduled services after the months of hesitation, concern and delay from Covid-19. It's sort of like hitting the reset button on a computer, which restores the settings to how they came from the factory. We are excited to go back to church. After all, remembering the Sabbath is the 4th Commandment (**Exodus 20:8**). You know, when we accept JESUS CHRIST as our Savior, HE hits the "reset button" on our sin nature, adds Grace to our "factory settings" and extends our useful life to eternity. How awesome is that? Let GOD reset you today!

Key Bible Verse

Exodus 20:8 - "Remember the Sabbath day by keeping it Holy."

Prayers & Notes

_____

_____

_____

_____

_____

_____

A Blessing from Yesterday _____

Something I am Thankful for Today _____

August 10

If you have a daughter or granddaughter, I am sure they and you saw the Disney movie Frozen (they've probably seen it multiple times on TV). One of the popular songs, "Some Things never change," is about the positive things we can count on staying the same during changing times. Today, we live in ever-changing times but, as Christians, we can count on GOD's WORD never changing. **Luke 21:33**. GOD's Love, HIS protection, and HIS promises of eternal life to those who believe will never change. Yes, GOD's WORD is unchangeable, but it is capable of changing everything. Can I hear an Amen?

✝

Key Bible Verse

Luke 21:33 – "Heaven and earth will pass away, but my words will never pass away."

Prayers & Notes

_____

_____

_____

_____

_____

_____

A Blessing from Yesterday _____

Something I am Thankful for Today _____

August 11

Our world has been turned upside down this year because so many people are afraid of a virus. Remember, fear is an emotion that does not come from GOD. The first evidence of fear in the Bible is in **Genesis 3:10** when Adam, after sinning, says "I was afraid." You see, fear is an emotion, and the only thing that can overcome it is Faith. Faith, by the way, requires action. Did you know that the Bible has "fear not" written 365 times? Yes, that's one for each day of the year, so it must be important. Work on your Faith, and you will get rid of fear. Praise HIM today!

Key Bible Verse

Genesis 3:10 – "He answered, "I heard you in the garden, and I was afraid because I was naked; so I hid."

Prayers & Notes

_____

_____

_____

_____

_____

A Blessing from Yesterday _____

Something I am Thankful for Today _____

Patrick E. Moore

August 12

I started thinking about circles this morning. One of GOD's perfect shapes, circles have been drawn since the beginning of recorded history, probably because of the shape of the sun and moon. Circles are in nature, astronomy, math, architecture, art, etc. It's the shape that represents eternity with no beginning and no end. **Psalms 34:7** says we have a circle of protection around us when we pray. Maybe we need to pray more, huh?

✝

Key Bible Verse

Psalms 34:7 – "he angel of the LORD encamps around those who fear him, and he delivers them"

Prayers & Notes

_____

_____

_____

_____

_____

_____

_____

A Blessing from Yesterday _____

Something I am Thankful for Today _____

August 13

There are billions of people on this earth seeking and searching for something that will love them, satisfy them, protect them, and promise ~~not~~ to never leave them. Most have either looked in the wrong place or rejected it when they found it. They are looking for JESUS. An international ministry I am involved in has had over 500,000 seekers a day hit their websites... looking for...seeking...HIM. Christians, we need to help those seekers by pronouncing and living our lives proudly and boldly for CHRIST. Do it today! **Ephesians 3:12**.

Key Bible Verse

Ephesians 3:12 – "In him and through faith in him we may approach God with freedom and confidence."

Prayers & Notes

_____

_____

_____

_____

_____

A Blessing from Yesterday _____

Something I am Thankful for Today _____

Patrick E. Moore

August 14

The early morning, when it's quiet, is no doubt my favorite part of the day. Why? Because it doesn't matter that yesterday, which may have been filled with struggles, darkness, frustration or pain, is gone. That was yesterday. Today is a new day, and GOD's Mercies begin anew once again. **Lamentations 3:22-23** was written when times were hard, and the people needed the promise from GOD that ~~we~~ they would have peace in their hearts forever. We still need HIS Mercies each morning to fight the daily battles we may be facing. May you start this day with praise and prayer to GOD.

✝

Key Bible Verse

Lamentations 3:22-23 – "Because of the LORD's great love we are not consumed, for his compassions never fail. They are new every morning; great is your faithfulness."

Prayers & Notes

_____

_____

_____

_____

_____

A Blessing from Yesterday _____

Something I am Thankful for Today _____

August 15

From the time we were infants all the way up to high school age, we needed a provider, didn't we? I contend that even though we are grown, we still need a provider. **Philippians 4:19** says our GOD is our Provider for everything we need, but there is a catch. We must ask HIM for it. Need healing? Ask Him. Need direction? Ask HIM. Need Peace? Ask HIM. Need comfort? Ask HIM. Whatever the need, ask HIM. Don't let your pride stand in the way of what GOD wants to do for you today. Humble yourself before your Heavenly FATHER this day!

Key Bible Verse

Philippians 4:19 – "And my God will meet all your needs according to the riches of his glory in Christ Jesus."

Prayers & Notes

_____

_____

_____

_____

_____

_____

A Blessing from Yesterday _____

Something I am Thankful for Today _____

August 16

As I was growing up, I remember hearing the quote "if it's worth having, then it's worth fighting for," and frankly, I can't remember what that thing was. As I have gotten older, I think that thing is love. GOD has given us people in our lives, both family and friends, to love whether they want or deserve it. After all, love is a blessing from GOD. Remember, HE loves us even though we don't deserve it, and His love will never change or ever leave us. **Romans 8:38-39.** Now, that is a model for us loving others, right? Therefore, fight for your relationships; they are worth fighting for.

✝

Key Bible Verse

Romans 8:38-39 – "For I am convinced that neither death nor life, neither angels nor demons, neither the present nor the future, nor any powers, neither height nor depth, nor anything else in all creation, will be able to separate us from the love of God that is in Christ Jesus our Lord."

Prayers & Notes

_____

_____

_____

_____

_____

A Blessing from Yesterday _____

Something I am Thankful for Today _____

August 17

Do you think it's fair to say that our parents and their parents lived quieter, more humble lives built around community? It was before the "what's in it for me" movement. Today, we are centered more on "self" than community. Even as Christians, we spend more time telling people we are "born again" and forget what we are born into. The Apostle Paul tells the church at Thessalonica "how to live among the pagans" in a way that they see your honorable deeds so they will Glorify GOD when HE comes again. In other words, stop seeking fame and accolades, and start leading others to CHRIST. That will be your greatest accomplishment.

Key Bible Verse

I Thessalonians 4:1 – "As for other matters, brothers and sisters, we instructed you how-to live-in order to please God, as in fact you are living. Now we ask you and urge you in the Lord Jesus to do this more and more."

Prayers & Notes

_____

_____

_____

_____

_____

A Blessing from Yesterday _____

Something I am Thankful for Today _____

Patrick E. Moore

August 18

Do you consider yourself to be a strategic or pragmatic personality, meaning you always have a strategy for your life or live life reasonably and logically? "Strategic" and "pragmatic" are not the same, but both are qualities to have. The dilemma is the road of life is not always straight and flat. No, life's journey has curves, mountains and unexpected detours, and you will need a foundation of faith when things go wrong. Here is a great quote I heard during Bible Study yesterday: "we need to be prayerful, before being strategic." Paul says it well in **Ephesians 6:18**, "pray in the Spirit at all times on all occasions.". Let this day be filled with prayer, so GOD will be a part of your plans.

Key Bible Verse

Ephesians 6:18 – "And pray in the Spirit on all occasions with all kinds of prayers and requests. With this in mind, be alert and always keep on praying for all the Lord's people."

Prayers & Notes

_____

_____

_____

_____

_____

A Blessing from Yesterday _____

Something I am Thankful for Today _____

August 19

We have all heard and probably used the phrase "as a last resort" refers to the only remaining, and least desirable, option when all else has failed. Too many times people, even Christians, turn to GOD as a last resort when they come face to face with a struggle. Here is the Good News...HE will be there. The Better News is we can turn to our Heavenly FATHER before the struggle, during the good times. **Psalms 62:8** says, "Trust in HIM always, pour out your heart before HIM, GOD is our refuge. Trust HIM today.

†

Key Bible Verse

Psalms 62:8 – "Trust in him at all times, you people; pour out your hearts to him, for God is our refuge."

Prayers & Notes

_____

_____

_____

_____

_____

_____

A Blessing from Yesterday _____

Something I am Thankful for Today _____

August 20

Did you know that there are over ten billion mobile connections in the world today? That is almost two for every human on earth. Unbelievable, huh? The average time people spend on their devices is about three hours each day or 1095 hours each year. That is enough time to listen to the Bible on audio fifteen times every year. According to Global Media Outreach, the world's largest online Christian ministry, mobile devices could help fulfill the Great Commission from **Matthew 28:18-19.** Ask God for some discipline to shift a portion of that time spent on mobile devices to GOD's WORD, and you will be Blessed because of it. #GodisGreat

Key Bible Verse

2 Timothy 4:7 – "I have fought the good fight, I have finished the race, I have kept the faith."

Prayers & Notes

_____

_____

_____

_____

_____

A Blessing from Yesterday _____

Something I am Thankful for Today _____

August 22

This morning, I received a weather alert on my smart watch warning me of a storm that was coming. Immediately, I thought of how cool it would be if GOD sent me a similar alert warning me of temptation or impending danger coming. I then remembered, GOD sent Christians a help and alarm system in the HOLY SPIRIT. God gave us the HOLY SPIRIT to guard us from evil, temptation, and sin. **John 14:26**. Every time you are faced with a situation or decision of right and wrong, the HOLY SPIRIT is what stirs inside your mind to warn you of danger. We must stay in GOD's WORD, so the HOLY SPIRIT can stay activated. Praise GOD!

Key Bible Verse

John. 14:26 – "But the Advocate, the Holy Spirit, whom the Father will send in my name, will teach you all things and will remind you of everything I have said to you."

Prayers & Notes

_____

_____

_____

_____

_____

A Blessing from Yesterday _____

Something I am Thankful for Today _____

Patrick E. Moore

August 23

Last night, we were coming home from dinner on a dark, two-lane winding road. I was so glad that the guard rails in the curves had bright orange reflectors that my headlights lit up to keep me safely on the road. It reminded me that GOD's WORD acts as reflectors on our road of life when we find ourselves going in an unfamiliar dark direction. If we read and obey GOD'S WORD, His radiance will light those dangerous curves we encounter and keep us safe. **Isaiah 41:10**. Fear not, brothers and sisters. GOD is with us always if you know HIM. Do you?

Key Bible Verse

Isaiah 41:10 – "So do not fear, for I am with you; do not be dismayed, for I am your God. I will strengthen you and help you; I will uphold you with my righteous right hand"

Prayers & Notes

_____

_____

_____

_____

_____

A Blessing from Yesterday _____

Something I am Thankful for Today _____

August 24

GOD used Moses to lead the people of Israel out of bondage, into the desert, across the Red Sea, and into the wilderness before they reached the Promised Land. That story in the Bible is amazing and encouraging because we all either have been, are, or will go through a wilderness experience during life. Here is the good News: "GOD will make a way when there seems to be no way." **Isaiah 43:19**. Fear not, GOD will not leave you in the desert. Remember, your destination is the Promised Land.

Key Bible Verse

Isaiah 43:19 – "See, I am doing a new thing! Now it springs up; do you not perceive it? I am making a way in the wilderness and streams in the wasteland."

Prayers & Notes

_____

_____

_____

_____

_____

_____

_____

A Blessing from Yesterday _____

Something I am Thankful for Today _____

Patrick E. Moore

August 25

We all need healing, either physical, emotional, or spiritual, and many of us need it right now. Did you know that the words you say to yourself or others will improve your healing or hinder it? What kind of words? Positive words help and negative words hinder healing. The Bible teaches this concept in **Proverbs 16:24** when it says "gracious words will heal our bones," and there are over 100 other verses about healing that support this statement. Also, it has been proved scientifically that negative words limit the healing part of our brain (check out a book written by Dr. Andrew Newberg, entitled "Words can Change the Brain"). Speak positive words to yourself and others, and encourage your family and friends to join in. Isn't GOD awesome?

Key Bible Verse

Proverbs 16:24 – "Gracious words are a honeycomb, sweet to the soul and healing to the bones."

Prayers & Notes

_____

_____

_____

_____

_____

A Blessing from Yesterday _____

Something I am Thankful for Today _____

August 26

Here is a wise tip, probably from someone's Mom. "To heal your wound, you must stop touching it." That is profound for all types of healing. Our wounds of life may leave pain, damage or scars, but we should stop focusing on them. Healing means the pain no longer controls us. In **Philippians 3:13-14**, Paul writes, "forgetting what is behind and reaching forward to what is ahead," which is our calling in CHRIST JESUS. Trust GOD and let HIM begin the healing today.

✝

Key Bible Verse

Philippians 3:13-14 – "Brothers and sisters, I do not consider myself yet to have taken hold of it. But one thing I do: Forgetting what is behind and straining toward what is ahead, I press on toward the goal to win the prize for which God has called me heavenward in Christ Jesus."

Prayers & Notes

_____

_____

_____

_____

_____

A Blessing from Yesterday _____

Something I am Thankful for Today _____

August 27

We all have been wounded during our lives, some many times. Wounds can come from bad choices, accidents, poor decisions and just because we live in a fallen world. When wounds occur, we have a choice. We can walk around with the wound unhealed and use it as a victim card or seek healing from GOD's promises. Yes, the scars will remain, but JESUS had scars when HE appeared to the Disciples after HIS Resurrection. Don't hide or be embarrassed by the scars. Use them as a reminder to you and others about GOD's healing power. **1 Peter 2:24**

✝

Key Bible Verse

1 Peter 2:24 - "He himself bore our sins" in his body on the cross, so that we might die to sins and live for righteousness; "by his wounds you have been healed."

Prayers & Notes

_____

_____

_____

_____

_____

_____

A Blessing from Yesterday _____

Something I am Thankful for Today _____

August 28

I guess all children like the game "Hide and Seek." I know I did; especially when I picked the perfect place and couldn't be found. Sometimes we still play that game with GOD before, during, or after we wander off the path of righteousness. Reality Check: we can't hide from GOD! HE sees, hears and knows everything about us, and thankfully, HE still loves us, protects us and promises us Eternal Life in spite of our goof ups. **1 John 1:9**. The next time you wander away from HIM, pray, ask for forgiveness and thank HIM for protecting you. HE will always be there with waiting arms. What a loving Heavenly FATHER we have.

Key Bible Verse

1 John 1:9 – "If we confess our sins, he is faithful and just and will forgive us our sins and purify us from all unrighteousness."

Prayers & Notes

_____

_____

_____

_____

_____

A Blessing from Yesterday _____

Something I am Thankful for Today _____

Patrick E. Moore

August 29

Elastic was first used in gloves, socks, suspenders and other fabrics around 1822. Our quality of life would be much different if we didn't have the stretching nature of elastic. Certainly, my pants and shorts would not fit as well as they do now. It got me to thinking that even though GOD's WORD does not change, our Faith needs to be stretched as we grow to mature Christians. Even the apostles asked JESUS to increase their Faith in **Luke 17:5**. Stretch your Faith today with the reading of GOD's WORD.

Key Bible Verse

Luke 17:5 – "The apostles said to the Lord, "Increase our faith!"

Prayers & Notes

_____

_____

_____

_____

_____

_____

_____

A Blessing from Yesterday _____

Something I am Thankful for Today _____

August 30

This morning, as I sit on the back porch, I am enjoying the gentle rain that is falling on our thirsty grass, trees and plants. Thank you, FATHER, for the needed rain. I notice the water beading up on the deck planks that have been treated with water repellant stain. We have to treat the deck on a regular basis for it to work well. This provides a good analogy for us and reminds me that if we allow our hearts and minds to be treated with GOD's WORD and teachings, then we can repel the temptation and sin that Satan tries to rain down on us. **James 4:7**. Thank HIM today!

Key Bible Verse

James 4:7 – "Submit yourselves, then, to God. Resist the devil, and he will flee from you."

Prayers & Notes

_____

_____

_____

_____

_____

_____

A Blessing from Yesterday _____

Something I am Thankful for Today _____

August 31

"Back to the Future" was a popular movie series in the mid 1980's. Marty McFly had a time machine car that could travel in back and forth in time. The movie's concept made me think about time in general. Yesterday is the day before today, right? It could be used in a context to mean all time in the past. Tomorrow is the day after today, right? But that could be used in the context of all time in the future. Sometimes we regret the past and fret about the future, don't we? As Christians, we are to focus on what is eternal, which is JESUS. Eternal means "never ceasing." Focus on HIM today and your regrets from yesterday will fade and HE will give you hope for the future. **Jeremiah 29:11.**

Key Bible Verse

Jeremiah 29:11 – "For I know the plans I have for you," Declares the Lord, "plans to prosper you and not to harm you, plans to give you hope and a future."

Prayers & Notes

_____

_____

_____

_____

_____

A Blessing from Yesterday _____

Something I am Thankful for Today _____

September 1

Identity theft has affected approximately fifteen million people in the last year and caused over $1.7 billion dollars in loss to individuals. Protecting your identity has never been as important as it is today from a financial standpoint. Speaking of identity, other than your name and address, who do others say you are? Will they describe you with your achievements and status or your witness for CHRIST? Remember, as Christians, our identity is not in what we have done, but what HE has done in us. **2 Timothy 2:19**. Thank HIM today!

Key Bible Verse

2 Timothy 2:19 – "Nevertheless, God's solid foundation stands firm, sealed with this inscription: "The Lord knows those who are his," and, "Everyone who confesses the name of the Lord must turn away from wickedness."

Prayers & Notes

_____

_____

_____

_____

_____

A Blessing from Yesterday _____

Something I am Thankful for Today _____

Patrick E. Moore

September 2

Because of my love of trains, I always notice train horns and know their meanings. Two long, one short, one long blast means the train is approaching a crossing, and one long blast means the train is approaching a station and not stopping. I heard that one long blast from a train yesterday. This morning, I am reminded of another horn that will someday blow announcing that the kingdom of the world will become the Kingdom of the LORD, and CHRIST will reign forever and ever. **Revelation 11:15**. May each train horn you hear remind you that CHRIST is coming back. Seek HIM so you are prepared.

Key Bible Verse

Revelation 11:15 – "The seventh angel sounded his trumpet, and there were loud voices in heaven, which said: "The kingdom of the world has become the kingdom of our Lord and of his Messiah, and he will reign for ever and ever."

Prayers & Notes

_____

_____

_____

_____

_____

A Blessing from Yesterday _____

Something I am Thankful for Today _____

September 3

What is a testimony? Well, the Latin root of the word testimony is "testis" which means "witness." A witness is someone who has seen, heard, or has evidence of the facts of a matter. According to **1 John 5:10**, we who believe in the SON of GOD have HIS testimony inside of us. Praise GOD! Now, we are called to share that testimony with others, right? Sometimes that can be hard, huh? The easiest way is to share what GOD has done in your life and how HE changed you. The fruits of your labor will either validate your testimony, or they won't. Share HIM with others today!

Key Bible Verse

1 John 5:10 – "Whoever believes in the Son of God accepts this testimony. Whoever does not believe God has made him out to be a liar, because they have not believed the testimony God has given about his Son."

Prayers & Notes

_____

_____

_____

_____

_____

A Blessing from Yesterday _____

Something I am Thankful for Today _____

Patrick E. Moore

September 4

We are living in crazy times, aren't we? On top of that, we all have our individual battles of fighting off health issues, financial struggles, anxieties that cloud our mind, or trying to heal relationships. The Bible tells us, as Christians, our road home will not be easy, but JESUS did promise us that we would never be alone. **1 Chronicles 28:20**. Have Faith in that promise. GOD is with us always, even now. Trust HIM today!

Key Bible Verse

1 Chronicles 28:20 – "David also said to Solomon his son, "Be strong and courageous, and do the work. Do not be afraid or discouraged, for the LORD God, my God, is with you. He will not fail you or forsake you until all the work for the service of the temple of the LORD is finished."

Prayers & Notes

_____

_____

_____

_____

_____

_____

A Blessing from Yesterday _____

Something I am Thankful for Today _____

September 5

Sympathy is a Greek word from the 16th century. Syn = together, and pathos = feeling, such as from suffering. I heard that explanation from the movie "42," which is the true and inspirational story of Jackie Robinson, the first black player to break the color barrier in Major League Baseball Do yourself a favor and watch that movie. You won't regret it. **Galatians 6:2** says, "we are to bear one another's burdens, so to fulfill the law of CHRIST." Ask GOD to increase your sympathy for others. There are many people who are suffering today and need our support. Praise HIM!

Key Bible Verse

Galatians 6:2 – "Carry each other's burdens, and in this way you will fulfill the law of Christ."

Prayers & Notes

_____

_____

_____

_____

_____

_____

A Blessing from Yesterday _____

Something I am Thankful for Today _____

September 6

There is always something magical about seeing GOD's creation of a rainbow, isn't there? Seven colors in perfect order every time. Remember, seven in the Jewish culture represents completion and perfection. The rainbow is first mentioned in the first book of the Bible as a sign and reminder from GOD that HE will not use a flood to destroy the earth again. 4 judgment and mercy. But you may not know that a rainbow is also mentioned in the last book of the Bible. **Revelation 4:2-4 d**escribes a rainbow surrounding the JESUS on the Throne of GOD. Remember this when you see another rainbow. HE is a GOD of mercy for those who accept HIM as their Savior.

Key Bible Verse

Revelation 4:2-3 – "At once I was in the Spirit, and there before me was a throne in heaven with someone sitting on it. And the one who sat there had the appearance of jasper and ruby. A rainbow that shone like an emerald encircled the throne."

Prayers & Notes

_____

_____

_____

_____

A Blessing from Yesterday _____

Something I am Thankful for Today _____

September 7

Camping and living in tents is not for everybody. As a Boy Scout, I loved to camp, but my wife and girls would prefer a Holiday Inn. Yesterday, in Sunday school, we talked about a very important tent that was used during the forty-year wandering of GOD's people in the desert. The "Tent of Presence" was a tabernacle ("Mishkan" in Hebrew) which means "dwelling place." **Exodus 40:34**. GOD had instructed MOSES to give the people hope that GOD's presence would always be with them. After JESUS' resurrection, the Apostle John wrote to both Jews and Gentiles that the WORD (our Creator) through JESUS would dwell within us forever if we let HIM. **John 1:14.** Now that is Good News. Praise HIM!

Key Bible Verse

John 1:14 – "The Word became flesh and made his dwelling among us. We have seen his glory, the glory of the one and only Son, who came from the Father, full of grace and truth."

Prayers & Notes

_____

_____

_____

_____

A Blessing from Yesterday _____

Something I am Thankful for Today _____

Patrick E. Moore

September 8

The mornings are getting cooler and the days shorter as we approach the autumn equinox. "Equinox" is a Latin word meaning "equal night.". It signals the beginning of fall and a time when the entire earth has equal daylight and nighttime. The calendar we use is an Egyptian lunar calendar and was developed about the time of the Exodus. The moon is mentioned over forty times in the Bible starting in **Genesis 1:14** with its creation along with the sun and stars on day four. The covenant GOD made to David in **Psalms 89:37** is compared to the moon which will be "forever and always a witness in the heavens." Now, let the moon remind you of GOD's Faithfulness. It will be forever.

Key Bible Verse

Genesis 1:14 – "And God said, 'Let there be lights in the vault of the sky to separate the day from the night, and let them serve as signs to Mark sacred times, and days and years,'"

Prayers & Notes

_____

_____

_____

_____

A Blessing from Yesterday _____

Something I am Thankful for Today _____

No Mountain Too High   251

September 9

A business friend said something yesterday that was profound: "It may seem too good to be true, but it's not too good to be free." He was talking about his consulting business, but I knew immediately this also applied to our Christian Faith. We have the promise of salvation and eternal life, even though we are still sinners, but it was not free. No, Jesus paid it all! And even though eternal life is free to us, being a soldier for the cross doesn't mean it won't cost us something. JESUS reminded us that in **Luke 9:23**, "If any man come after me, let him deny himself and take up his cross daily, and follow me." Now, that's a price worth paying. I'm in; how about you? Praise HIM today!

Key Bible Verse

Luke 9:23 – "Then he said to them all: "Whoever wants to be my disciple must deny themselves and take up their cross daily and follow me."

Prayers & Notes

_____

_____

_____

_____

_____

A Blessing from Yesterday _____

Something I am Thankful for Today _____

Patrick E. Moore

September 10

We all have had moments or challenges in life that looked impossible to overcome, but somehow things worked out. Some people might say it was luck, good fortune, karma or chance, but we know the truth; it was GOD watching over us. This morning, I am reminded that there is nothing impossible with our GOD. **Matthew 19:26**. And yes, HE is mightiest when we are weak and weary. Praise HIM this morning and thank HIM for being our GOD for whom nothing is impossible. Don't give up, give in to HIM today!

✝

Key Bible Verse

Matthew 19:26 – "Jesus looked at them and said, "With man this is impossible, but with God all things are possible."

Prayers & Notes

_____

_____

_____

_____

_____

_____

_____

A Blessing from Yesterday _____

Something I am Thankful for Today _____

September 11

The definition of flawless is "without blemishes or imperfections; perfect or without any mistakes or shortcomings." That might be an ideal standard for product manufacturing or a realistic goal for gymnasts, but it's impossible for us to live an entire life that way. Remember there was only perfect man, and HIS name was JESUS. However, when we accept JESUS as our Savior, HE takes all of our blemishes, imperfections, mistakes and shortcomings, and by HIS Grace we are washed white as snow. **Psalms 51:7.** Flawless is how HE views us on the inside, so maybe we should clean ourselves up on the outside. Worship HIM and thank HIM for what He has done for you today!

Key Bible Verse

Psalms 51:7 – "Cleanse me with hyssop, and I will be clean; wash me, and I will be whiter than snow."

Prayers & Notes

_____

_____

_____

_____

_____

A Blessing from Yesterday _____

Something I am Thankful for Today _____

Patrick E. Moore

September 12

Carl Jung was a famous Swiss Psychiatrist born in 1875 who wrote several books on analytical psychology and how the mind works. His work revealed patterns of behavior and character traits referred to as archetypes, and he theorized we all have and need hero archetypes. Why? We need those people in our lives to aspire to and help us guide our moral selves. Marvel comics and movies have made a fortune creating mythical superheroes. The greatest "real" hero of all time was JESUS. He turns the hopeless into the hopeful, the fearful into the fearless, the unloving into the loving, and the weary into the rested. You just have to ask HIM into your heart. **Isaiah 40:31**. Now, that's a hero you want in your life.

Key Bible Verse

Isaiah 40:31 – "but those who hope in the Lord will renew their strength. They will soar on wings like eagles; they will run and not grow weary; they will walk and not be faint."

Prayers & Notes

_____

_____

_____

_____

A Blessing from Yesterday _____

Something I am Thankful for Today _____

September 13

Supersonic means going faster than the speed of sound which is 768 mph. That is considered Mach 1. A US Air Force test pilot from West Virginia and an acquaintance of my Dad was the first human to break the sound barrier. Later, also as fighter pilots, my twin brother and I had the thrill to fly faster than Mach 1. Today the space shuttle travels through space at over 17,000 mph. That's peanuts! GOD created our earth to travel through space at over 67,000 mph and, amazingly, our earth rotates on its axis at 1000 mph. Yes, that is over the speed over Mach 1! That's one 24,000-mile revolution every 24 hours. We don't sense it because of GOD's creation of gravity. Unbelievable, huh? **Psalms 47.2** says it best, "we have an awesome GOD." Whatever you are facing today, fear not. Our GOD's Power is available to you and me. Worship and Praise HIM today.

Key Bible Verse

Psalms 47.2 – "For the LORD Most High is awesome, the great King over all the earth."

Prayers & Notes

_____

_____

_____

_____

A Blessing from Yesterday _____

Something I am Thankful for Today _____

September 14

Creativity starts with our imagination. Some people seem to have that creativity gene, and some don't. But all of us have the temptation gene to sin, and it also starts with imagination. Remember, temptation doesn't come from GOD. **James 1:12**. Without GOD's WORD as our defense, rationalization may set in which could lead to sin. Blessed is the man that endures temptation. **James 1:12**. Pray for strength.

✝

Key Bible Verse

James 1:12 – "Blessed *is* the man who endures temptation; for when he has been approved, he will receive the crown of life which the Lord has promised to those who love Him."

Prayers & Notes

_____

_____

_____

_____

_____

_____

A Blessing from Yesterday _____

Something I am Thankful for Today _____

September 15

Do you know the computer term "GIGO," which stands for "garbage in-garbage out?" It implies the quality of output depends on the quality of input. Do you know the same thing is true for our minds? Neuroscience proves what you think changes your brain and body. Dr. Caroline Leaf's book, "Switch On your Brain", says we have the ability to improve our intelligence, happiness and health with the conscious effort to capture your positive thoughts and feelings. This concept is also Biblical, and I trust that source more than Leaf's book. Read Paul's words in **Romans 12:2**. Let GOD transform you into a new person by changing the way you think, then you will learn GOD's will for your life which is pleasing and perfect." Want a happier and healthier life? Ask GOD to help you change the way you think!

Key Bible Verse

Romans 12:2 – "Do not conform to the pattern of this world but be transformed by the renewing of your mind. Then you will be able to test and approve what God's will is—his good, pleasing and perfect will."

Prayers & Notes

_____

_____

_____

A Blessing from Yesterday _____

Something I am Thankful for Today _____

September 16

The ocean is sometimes called the "The Great Unknown" because there is so much we don't know about it. The average depth is 12,000 feet, and since light cannot penetrate water past 1000 feet, there is extreme darkness. Ocean plant life needs light to survive, which is why most marine life lives within the first 600 feet of water. Sometimes in life, we find ourselves in deep and dark waters due to a life struggle, and we find it hard to survive in the darkness. But there is Good News. GOD's Light can penetrate any darkness we might find ourselves in. **John 1:5.** GOD's WORD will lead you to The Light!

✝

Key Bible Verse

John 1:5 – "The light shines in the darkness, and the darkness has not overcome it."

Prayers & Notes

_____

_____

_____

_____

_____

A Blessing from Yesterday _____

Something I am Thankful for Today _____

September 17

Flying airplanes really taught me how to use a compass since every direction or heading I flew was based on a 360-degree compass. For example, if you turned 180 degrees, you would be going the opposite direction turning 180 degrees is what we must do when we forgive someone for their sin or repent of our own. Both involve a sin of some type that causes us to turn from GOD. Truly forgiving and repenting means we have to turn 180 degrees and reverse our feelings, actions and thoughts. The Apostle Paul tells us in **Acts 3:19** to turn towards GOD. If you need to forgive someone, repent to GOD for your transgressions, or if you have just found yourself wandering in the desert, turn 180 degrees back towards the HEAVENLY FATHER. HIS open arms are waiting.

Key Bible Verse

Acts 3:19 – "Repent, then, and turn to God, so that your sins may be wiped out, that times of refreshing may come from the Lord,"

Prayers & Notes

_____

_____

_____

_____

A Blessing from Yesterday _____

Something I am Thankful for Today _____

Patrick E. Moore

September 18

When our grandkids were little, they all loved to romp in the backyard creek and get all wet and nasty. We often made them strip out of their wet clothes in the garage then sent them to the shower or bath to get scrubbed clean. You know, as a child of GOD, it is comforting to know that no matter how messy I may get from falling in life's mud puddles, My Heavenly FATHER will scrub me with HIS Grace and Mercy to make me clean again. **1 John 1:7**. Here is some Good News: it doesn't matter how filthy you may be, GOD's Grace and Mercy can make you white as snow. Thank HIM today!

Key Bible Verse

1 John 1:7 – "But if we walk in the light, as he is in the light, we have fellowship with one another, and the blood of Jesus, his Son, purifies us from all sin."

Prayers & Notes

_____

_____

_____

_____

_____

A Blessing from Yesterday _____

Something I am Thankful for Today _____

September 19

You have heard the expression "being at the right place at the right time," right? It's an old expression that suggests luck or happenstance regarding events. As I get older, I am more convinced that there is no happenstance, but that GOD directs our steps, always. **Psalms 37:23**. The story of a man named Zacchaeus climbing a tree in Jericho just to see JESUS is a good example. JESUS saw Zacchaeus in the tree, called him down and Zacchaeus repented and received salvation. Some might say Zacchaeus was lucky to climb that particular tree. I say GOD knew that day would come and had the tree grow in that exact spot. GOD has already planted trees we will climb one day. Trust HIM Always!

Key Bible Verse

Psalms 37:23 – "The LORD makes firm the steps of the one who delights in him;"

Prayers & Notes

_____

_____

_____

_____

_____

A Blessing from Yesterday _____

Something I am Thankful for Today _____

Patrick E. Moore

September 20

Studies say that we need a minimum of seven hours of rest or more each night to maintain a healthy life. I can attest to that. As I get older, I need a little more than seven hours and maybe an additional nap. But our real rest comes from the LORD when we become one of HIS Children. Yes, it is true, so turn over all your concerns and fears before you go to bed. HE is going to be up anyway. Yes, our GOD never sleeps nor slumbers as the author sings in **Psalms 121:3-4.** Whether we are awake or sleeping, our LORD is fighting Satan and his evil minions on our behalf (because evil doesn't sleep either). Seek HIM and rest knowing HE has your back.

Key Bible Verse

Psalms 121:3-4 – "He will not let your foot slip— he who watches over you will not slumber; indeed, he who watches over Israel will neither slumber nor sleep."

Prayers & Notes

_____

_____

_____

_____

A Blessing from Yesterday _____

Something I am Thankful for Today _____

September 21

Even though we live in a polarized world with conflicting thoughts on everything from church to politics, there is something that we all have in common. Yes, I said in common. We are all born in the image of GOD according to **Genesis 1:26-27**. This means we all are born with a sense of fairness, goodness and love. You might call it our moral compass. Even atheists can't answer the question of "where did your sense of right and wrong come from?" Our moral compass can get out of calibration due to pride, fear or our sinful nature. The best way to make sure it is pointing back towards righteousness is to SEEK OUR heavenly FATHER through prayer and the study of HIS WORD. Thank HIM today!

Key Bible Verse

Genesis 1:26-27 – "Then God said, "Let us make mankind in our image, in our likeness, so that they may rule over the fish in the sea and the birds in the sky, over the livestock and all the wild animals, and over all the creatures that move along the ground." So God created mankind in his own image, in the image of God he created them; male and female he created them."

Prayers & Notes

_____

_____

_____

A Blessing from Yesterday _____

Something I am Thankful for Today _____

Patrick E. Moore

September 22

As a kid, my Mom did not like for us to use the phrase "I can't." She was always trying to instill in us that anything was possible if we set our minds to it. That encouragement created confidence in us and is part of her legacy. You know, in life, sometimes we face things that just seem impossible, and if we depend on our own strength and ability, they are. The Bible is full of these kinds of stories. Read about Abraham and Sarah, Noah, Moses, Mary and Joseph, Lazarus and others. All of these stories were impossible alone, but GOD made them possible. Yesterday, we were studying **Matthew 19** and in **verse 26**, it says "But Jesus beheld them, and said unto them, with men this is impossible; but with God all things are possible." Facing the impossible today? Remember, with GOD, anything is possible. Have a great day.

✝

Key Bible Verse

Matthew 19:26 – "Jesus looked at them and said, "With man this is impossible, but with God all things are possible."

Prayers & Notes

_____

_____

_____

_____

A Blessing from Yesterday _____

Something I am Thankful for Today _____

September 23

Recently I read about the walls around Constantinople which protected the Roman capital from all sieges for over 800 years. Amazing, huh? Sometimes in life we build imaginary walls around our jobs, relationships or family in hopes we won't have to deal with something that might cause us pain or disappointment. Remember, walls are built because of fear of something or someone. Face those fears and listen to GOD's directions. It worked for Joshua and GOD's People at the walls of Jericho. **Joshua 6:20**. They shouted, and the walls came tumbling down so they could enter the Promised Land. Sounds like a good plan as we face our walls, huh? Shout to the LORD today!

Key Bible Verse

Joshua 6:20 – "When the trumpets sounded, the army shouted, and at the sound of the trumpet, when the men gave a loud shout, the wall collapsed; so everyone charged straight in, and they took the city."

Prayers & Notes

_____

_____

_____

_____

_____

A Blessing from Yesterday _____

Something I am Thankful for Today _____

Patrick E. Moore

September 24

I have a few bricks on the edge of my front steps that are coming loose and need some new mortar to repair them. As I was looking online for types of mortar to buy, I ran across an interesting definition for mortar: "a substance used for uniting brick or stone to buildings". "Uniting." Hmm... That is a perfect description of its purpose to secure bricks together. It makes me think that GOD's Church is made up of people (the bricks), and what unites or binds us together is Love. Yes, Love is the mortar that holds together any family, **Colossians 3:14**. Think about your own family. If some of your bricks are coming loose, maybe you need a little more love to unite them stronger. Share a little more love with your family today. It will make GOD smile.

✝

Key Bible Verse

Colossians 3:14 – "And over all these virtues put on love, which binds them all together in perfect unity."

Prayers & Notes

_____

_____

_____

_____

_____

A Blessing from Yesterday _____

Something I am Thankful for Today _____

September 25

Webster's definition of theology is "the study of GOD and GOD's relation to the world." Many Christian theologians worry that theology is declining in the U.S and Britain while increasing on other continents like Africa, India, and Asia. One of their proving points is that there are more Anglicans in church in Nigeria on any given Sunday than there are in the U.S. and Britain combined. Wow, can you believe that? What is your theology? Has it changed over the years? Here is something to consider. Everything we say and do is our theology and our view of GOD. Want others to know that you know JESUS? Maybe it's time to start talking and doing the things of GOD...everyday...as proclaimed by HIS WORD. **Matthew 5:16**. Praise HIM Today!

Key Bible Verse

Matthew 5:16 – "In the same way, let your light shine before others, that they may see your good deeds and glorify your Father in heaven."

Prayers & Notes

_____

_____

_____

_____

A Blessing from Yesterday _____

Something I am Thankful for Today _____

September 26

"Pulling back the curtain" is an expression that means "to reveal the truth." The old classic movie, "The Wizard of OZ", comes to mind. Sometimes in life, we face difficult circumstances, and we wonder if we can survive what's ahead of us. This is part of the spiritual battles we will face during our life, but remember, GOD is with us. GOD shows us a powerful glimpse of the spiritual realm in the Bible story of King Anan in **2 Kings 6:17-18**. The King woke to find his enemy army surrounding HIS city. Elisha prayer that GOD would open HIS eyes so HE could see the army of Angels and chariots sent by GOD to defeat the Kings enemy. He did! If we could pull back the curtains of Heaven, we would see that GOD has HIS hand in all the battles of life. Trust HIM. HE IS WITH US!

✝

Key Bible Verse

2 Kings 6:17-18 – "And Elisha prayed, 'Open his eyes, Lord, so that he may see.' Then the Lord opened the servant's eyes, and he looked and saw the hills full of horses and chariots of fire all around Elisha. As the enemy came down toward him, Elisha prayed to the Lord, 'Strike this army with blindness.' So he struck them with blindness, as Elisha had asked."

Prayers & Notes

_____

_____

_____

A Blessing from Yesterday _____

Something I am Thankful for Today _____

September 27

I know that some of you who are reading these thoughts this morning is hurting emotionally, have a scary diagnosis, or are hurting from a sickness or injury. I am so sorry. It's human to ask, "Why me?" or "What now?" The origin of something bad in your life doesn't come from GOD, because only good comes from GOD (**James 1:17**). Evil comes from the fall in the Garden of Eden. What now? Speak to the evil in your life and command it to leave, in the name of JESUS. Isaiah Says, "By HIS stripes, we are healed." Speak to your pain with Faith, and let GOD give you Peace every day!

Key Bible Verse

James 1:17 – "Every good and perfect gift is from above, coming down from the Father of the heavenly lights, who does not change like shifting shadows."

Prayers & Notes

_____

_____

_____

_____

_____

A Blessing from Yesterday _____

Something I am Thankful for Today _____

Patrick E. Moore

September 28

What does it mean to never give up on someone? It means that your love and forgiveness is so strong that it overcomes pain and disappointment. It should be a natural thing for a parent and good friend, but sometimes our pride and ego get in the way. Thank goodness, our Heavenly FATHER never gives up on us. **Joshua 1:9** says, "we need to be strong and courageous, because GOD will always be with us." Have you given up on someone? Maybe it's time to rethink that stance. Have a Blessed day!

✝

Key Bible Verse

Joshua 1:9 – "Have I not commanded you? Be strong and courageous. Do not be afraid; do not be discouraged, for the Lord your God will be with you wherever you go."

Prayers & Notes

_____

_____

_____

_____

_____

_____

A Blessing from Yesterday _____

Something I am Thankful for Today _____

September 29

Whenever you are having any doubt about GOD's presence in your life, get up early and face east so you can watch the sunrise GOD promises us each day. Sometimes we let doubt creep in regarding, peace, comfort, healing, etc., but those things are just as sure for Christians as the promise of a sunrise. The only difference is in the timing, but rest assured, GOD'S TIMING will be perfect. Thank you, FATHER, for letting me view your sunrise this morning. **Psalms 118:24.** "Let us rejoice and be glad in it." Don't doubt GOD's promises. They arise each day like the sunrise.

✝

Key Bible Verse

Psalms 118:24 – "The Lord has done it this very day; let us rejoice today and be glad."

Prayers & Notes

_____

_____

_____

_____

_____

_____

A Blessing from Yesterday _____

Something I am Thankful for Today _____

Patrick E. Moore

September 30

While waiting on another sunrise from my hotel balcony, I started watching a lone fisherman on the beach. Based on the number of rods, the large ice chest and wagon full of gear, I determined this was no amateur fisherman but an experienced local. Watching him throw a cast net really caught my attention. He was using it to catch small fish to use as bait. I immediately thought of JESUS walking beside the Sea of Galilee and seeing Andrew and his brother Peter casting their nets. In **Mark 1:16**, JESUS says to them, "follow ME and become fishers of men." That is what we all are called to do, right? Cast the net of GOD's WORD and Truth so others may know HIM. Are you up for the challenge? Happy fishing today!

✝

Key Bible Verse

Mark 1:16 – "As Jesus walked beside the Sea of Galilee, he saw Simon and his brother Andrew casting a net into the lake, for they were fishermen."

Prayers & Notes

_____

_____

_____

_____

_____

A Blessing from Yesterday _____

Something I am Thankful for Today _____

October 1

Where does the sand come from? Over eons, the waves of the ocean pulverize the rocks and shells to form the sand. The white sands of the gulf coast come from tiny bits of quartz washed down from the Appalachian Mountains. Interesting, huh? Some say there are therapeutic benefits to walking on the sand due to the earth's negative ions. Walking barefoot allows the vast network of nerves in our feet, to be stimulated. In **Psalms 139:18**, David thanks GOD for HIS loving thoughts which are immeasurable, like the grains of sand on the earth. Want GOD's love "to infinity and beyond?" Surrender to HIM today!

Key Bible Verse

Psalms 139:18 – "Were I to count them, they would outnumber the grains of sand— when I awake, I am still with you."

Prayers & Notes

_____

_____

_____

_____

_____

A Blessing from Yesterday _____

Something I am Thankful for Today _____

Patrick E. Moore

October 2

While walking on the beach yesterday, we came across an elegant bird that seemed to be posing for the passersby. The bird was the Great Egret, a member of the Heron family. A local bird watcher said it was a rare site in southeast Florida. It nearly became extinct in the 1800's from the harvesting of the fine plumes they grow during mating season. They are very patient birds who wait for their prey to walk or swim by them. Then, with their long necks, razor sharp beaks and lightning reflexes, they capture their prey. Through their patience, GOD provides. Why can't we, as Christians, be more patient with the world and more hopeful about Christ providing for us? Let us pray for more patience today. **James 5:8**

✝

Key Bible Verse

James 5:8 – "You too, be patient and stand firm, because the Lord's coming is near."

Prayers & Notes

_____

_____

_____

_____

A Blessing from Yesterday _____

Something I am Thankful for Today _____

October 3

The journey and transformation of a caterpillar into a butterfly is called meta-morphosis. It is an incredible example of GOD's amazing life cycle and is probably the favorite biology study for school-aged kids. I know it was for me. The word metamorphosis, of Greek origin, is very applicable to our spiritual journey. It is mentioned four times in the Bible and is translated into "transformed." In **Romans 12:1-2**, Paul tells the new believers that because of GOD's Mercy and Grace, they have been transformed and should live a life of service, honoring our Heavenly FATHER. This metamorphosis begins with the renewing of our minds through prayer and the reading of GOD's WORD. May your inner butterfly project GOD's beauty to others today!

Key Bible Verse

Romans 12:1-2 – "Therefore, I urge you, brothers and sisters, in view of God's mercy, to offer your bodies as a living sacrifice, holy and pleasing to God—this is your true and proper worship. Do not conform to the pattern of this world but be transformed by the renewing of your mind. Then you will be able to test and approve what God's will is—his good, pleasing and perfect will."

Prayers & Notes

_____

_____

_____

A Blessing from Yesterday _____

Something I am Thankful for Today _____

Patrick E. Moore

October 4

There have been multiple studies of people instructed to walk a straight line while blindfolded. In every case, the subjects end up walking in circles. This has baffled scientists for years. Without a fixed-point reference point like the sun, moon or a mountaintop, we cannot walk in a straight line unless we use a compass or GPS. You see, this is also true for our Christian Walk. It is not good enough to have a goal to be good, righteous and GODLY. Without the reference point of GOD and HIS WORD, there is no way to walk in a righteous straight line. We would wander spiritually in circles. **Proverbs 3:6** instructs us to "in all ways acknowledge HIM, and he will make our paths straight." Let GOD be your compass today and forever!

Key Bible Verse

Proverbs 3:6 – "in all your ways submit to him, and he will make your paths straight."

Prayers & Notes

_____

_____

_____

_____

A Blessing from Yesterday _____

Something I am Thankful for Today _____

October 5

The humps on a camel's back store fat that allows it to go long periods of time in the desert without nourishment. When depleted, the humps can sag and droop, but with renewed nourishment, they will go back to normal. God's WORD is the nourishment for our Christian Faith and Spirit, especially when we are going through a desert season of life. Without GOD's nourishment, our Faith and Spirit can also sag and droop. In **John 6:35,** JESUS declared "I am the bread of life. Whoever comes to me will not go hungry and whoever believes in me will not go thirsty." Seek the nourishment of GOD's WORD today!

Key Bible Verse

John 6:35 – "Then Jesus declared, "I am the bread of life. Whoever comes to me will never go hungry, and whoever believes in me will never be thirsty."

Prayers & Notes

_____

_____

_____

_____

_____

A Blessing from Yesterday _____

Something I am Thankful for Today _____

Patrick E. Moore

October 6

The pandemic we have experienced the last seven months has been difficult for everyone on so many fronts, especially in the loss of community. GOD did not create us to be loners but to be a part of a larger community that includes family, friends, our church, other believers, and also the community in which we live. The Bible is full of scriptures on why we need each other. We are called to encourage one another (**Hebrews 10:24-25**); to pray for one another for healing (**James 5:16**); to carry each other's burdens, (**Galatians 6:2**); to warn each other of sin (**1 Thessalonians 5:14**); and, maybe most important, to rejoice and mourn with each other (**Romans 12:15**). Don't let Satan separate you from the community of Believers. The decision is up to us.

Key Bible Verse

Romans 12:15 – "Rejoice with those who rejoice; mourn with those who mourn."

Prayers & Notes

_____

_____

_____

_____

A Blessing from Yesterday _____

Something I am Thankful for Today _____

October 7

Have you ever said or had someone say to you "I am going to keep my eye on you?" The expression might be positive or negative, but in either way, it's meant to only be for a short period of time. The Bible says our LORD and HEAVENLY FATHER keeps HIS eyes on the righteous and HIS ears attentive to their cry. **Psalms 34:15**. HE is watching out for us. Who are the righteous? You and me and all of those that have accepted HIM as LORD and SAVIOR. Don't worry, it doesn't mean we have to be perfect, because we can never achieve that. But because JESUS died on the cross for our sins, HE gives us HIS robe of righteousness to wear. Hallelujah and Amen.

Key Bible Verse

Psalms 34:15 – "The eyes of the LORD are on the righteous, and his ears are attentive to their cry;"

Prayers & Notes

_____

_____

_____

_____

_____

A Blessing from Yesterday _____

Something I am Thankful for Today _____

Patrick E. Moore

October 8

Remember when we had to use maps and written directions to take a trip or find someone's house? Trying to read a map with a flashlight at night while driving was an even more distracting than texting is today. There were many times I missed a road sign and ended up lost. That reminds me that sometimes while we are traveling the highway of life, there are unexpected detours that we have to take to get where we are going. GOD may be putting signposts along our path that we need to follow, so don't miss them. Maybe HE is directing you to a rest stop because you are weary, or maybe HE wants you to help someone. Stay in prayer with your Heavenly FATHER, follow HIS directions and you won't get lost. **Jeremiah 6:16**.

✝

Key Bible Verse

Jeremiah 6:16 – "This is what the Lord says: "Stand at the crossroads and look; ask for the ancient paths, ask where the good way is, and walk in it, and you will find rest for your souls. But you said, 'We will not walk in it.'

Prayers & Notes

_____

_____

_____

_____

A Blessing from Yesterday _____

Something I am Thankful for Today _____

October 9

There is no doubt that our western civilization today is busier than ever before. Technology allows us to connect with more people than ever, and our minds have more stimulation daily due to electronics. At the same time, Satan has used all of that to create loneliness and hopelessness at an alarming rate. How do I know? Statistics show that U.S. suicides are up 25% over the last ten years, especially among 15-24 years old. How tragic. Suicide is the 10th leading cause of death in the U.S. Having hope in something bigger than yourself is the only solution to that problem. Want to have a personal relationship with the ONE who will stay with you when the world walks away? Get to know JESUS! **Deuteronomy 31:6** says "Be strong and courageous. Do not fear or be in dread of them, for it is the Lord your God who goes with you. He will not leave you or forsake you." You are never alone.

Key Bible Verse

Deuteronomy 31:6 – "Be strong and courageous. Do not be afraid or terrified because of them, for the LORD your God goes with you; he will never leave you nor forsake you."

Prayers & Notes

_____

_____

_____

A Blessing from Yesterday _____

Something I am Thankful for Today _____

October 10

When it comes to being on time, there are only two types of people: those who always arrive early and those who always arrive late. What about those who are always on time? They are also early arrivers, but they stall or drive around because they don't want to be first and want to appear perfect. LOL. With all the electronic alarms and reminders we have, and Siri directing traffic, we should be better about being on time. Speaking of time, our Heavenly FATHER is the author of time. HE answers our prayers in HIS time, not ours, and it's always perfect timing. **Ecclesiastes 3:1**. Be earnest with your prayers today, but also be patient. Remember, you can trust your Heavenly FATHER to always be on time.

Key Bible Verse

Ecclesiastes 3:1 – "There is a time for everything, and a season for every activity under the heavens:"

Prayers & Notes

_____

_____

_____

_____

A Blessing from Yesterday _____

Something I am Thankful for Today _____

October 11

This morning, while traveling in the mountain area of East Tennessee, I noticed a small white steeple on a little church in the country. The vertical steeple of a Christian Church is an iconic symbol of church architecture that was introduced during the Georgian period. The style was developed in Europe during the reign of King George 1. Christian churches brought the architecture to America, and it remains a visual testimony today. **John 12:32** quotes JESUS as saying, "And I, when I am lifted up from the earth, will draw all people to myself."

May each church steeple you see remind you to lift JESUS up in your heart and prayers. Amen.

Key Bible Verse

John 12:32 – "And I, when I am lifted up from the earth, will draw all people to myself."

Prayers & Notes

_____

_____

_____

_____

A Blessing from Yesterday _____

Something I am Thankful for Today _____

October 12

We all have some physical scars from falls, sports, accidents or surgeries, and like me, you know the details of when and how they happened. I call them battle scars. It's amazing how GOD made our bodies to heal our wounds, isn't it? In addition, we may also have some invisible scars that may or may not have healed completely. They are emotional scars that come from trauma, losing a loved one, trials, or broken relationships. Even though people can't see them, we know they are there. GOD has created a solution for those scars, too, through HIS Son JESUS CHRIST. For the scar to be healed, start with prayer, then seek GOD's WORD for comfort, and then talk it through with someone you love and trust. Read **1 Peter 1:6-7** for a clear picture of trials and scars. GOD has a purpose for those scars too.

✝

Key Bible Verse

1 Peter 1:6-7 – "In all this you greatly rejoice, though now for a little while you may have had to suffer grief in all kinds of trials. These have come so that the proven genuineness of your faith—of greater worth than gold, which perishes even though refined by fire—may result in praise, glory and honor when Jesus Christ is revealed."

Prayers & Notes

_____

_____

_____

A Blessing from Yesterday _____

Something I am Thankful for Today _____

October 13

My twin brother and I loved the Boy Scouts when we were teenagers. We learned about hiking, camping, map reading and survival, etc., but that knowledge alone did not earn us merit badges. We had to complete the activities, too. We did both on our way to the rank of Eagle Scout. It's the same way with Faith and Works as Christians. Our Faith in GOD should lead us to a changed life – not a perfect one, but one that wants to do good works for others. Remember, knowledge of GOD alone doesn't cut it. Even Satan knew about GOD and shuddered. No, our Faith should produce the fruit of good works. Faith alone that has no good works is dead according to **James 2:14**. Let others see that fruit in you today.

Key Bible Verse

James 2:14 – "What good is it, my brothers and sisters, if someone claims to have faith but has no deeds? Can such faith save them?"

Prayers & Notes

_____

_____

_____

_____

A Blessing from Yesterday _____

Something I am Thankful for Today _____

Patrick E. Moore

October 14

This morning, while listening to Christian artist Zach Williams sing his popular song "Rescue Story," I started thinking about the rescue stories in the Bible. The definition of rescue is "the act of being saved from a dangerous situation or distress." There is the story of Daniel, rescued from lion's den, his friends from the fiery oven, and the Israelites at the Red Sea, just to name a few. But the greatest rescue story of all is our rescue (yes, you and me) from the pits of darkness to the realm of Glory by the Grace of GOD. As Zach sings in his song, "you were the voice in the desert, calling me out in the dead of night, fighting my battles for me." Yes, due to the blood of the cross, JESUS is our rescue story. **Psalms 107:19**. Thank HIM TODAY!

✝

Key Bible Verse

Psalms 107:19 – "Then they cried to the LORD in their trouble, and he saved them from their distress."

Prayers & Notes

_____

_____

_____

_____

_____

A Blessing from Yesterday _____

Something I am Thankful for Today _____

October 15

This morning during my prayer time, GOD convicted me to lift up those who are reading this daily thought. I know many are struggling with a variety of issues that are causing fear, pain, uncertainty, loneliness and maybe even hopelessness. Some are sick, some are awaiting scary tests results, some are facing marital problems, some are facing financial hurdles, and probably all of us are facing anxiety about the future of our country. Let me point you to the Bible and **Job 1:1**. Job was a man considered "blameless (of moral character), upright, who feared GOD and shunned evil", yet he suffered greatly during a season of life. But he made it through that season, and GOD restored everything and blessed him greatly. Don't give in to the fear of Satan. Lean on GOD today. HE is in control and will bring you through this season. Praise HIM.

✝

Key Bible Verse

Job 1:1 – "In the land of Uz there lived a man whose name was Job. This man was blameless and upright; he feared God and shunned evil."

Prayers & Notes

_____

_____

_____

_____

A Blessing from Yesterday _____

Something I am Thankful for Today _____

Patrick E. Moore

October 16

If you are having a problem with your physical vision, you probably need to go to an optometrist to see if you need new glasses or some other corrective action. Here is a question. Where do you go when you are having a problem with your spiritual vision? You see, without spiritual vision, you cannot see what direction to go to fulfill your spiritual destiny. GOD's WORD reveals the paths we should follow, and the HOLY SPIRIT illuminates what GOD has already revealed. **1 Corinthians 2:9-10.** Keep GOD's vision for your life front and center in your mind, so you don't get lost. May GOD help keep your spiritual vision at 20/20.

Key Bible Verse

1 Corinthians 2:9-10 – "However, as it is written: "What no eye has seen, what no ear has heard, and what no human mind has conceived"— the things God has prepared for those who love him— these are the things God has revealed to us by his Spirit. The Spirit searches all things, even the deep things of God."

Prayers & Notes

_____

_____

_____

_____

A Blessing from Yesterday _____

Something I am Thankful for Today _____

October 17

Did you know that bread is the most consumed food in the world? It has been made for thousands of years. Today's popular bread has only three main ingredients: flour, water and yeast. Leave one out, and you don't have bread. Similarly, for us as Christians, there are just a few ingredients we need to understand the Bible. You see, GOD's WORD is essential for our Christian growth. The first ingredient is personal understanding. We must read it and not solely depend on someone's interpretation first. The second ingredient is humility. We must approach GOD's WORD with a humble spirit that wants to learn. The third ingredient is the HOLY SPIRIT who is the embodiment of CHRIST himself and helps us learn. **Corinthians 2:12**. And just like that, GOD's WORD will nourish us always. Praise HIM Today.

✝

Key Bible Verse

1 Corinthians 2:12 – "What we have received is not the spirit of the world, but the Spirit who is from God, so that we may understand what God has freely given us.'

Prayers & Notes

_____

_____

_____

_____

A Blessing from Yesterday _____

Something I am Thankful for Today _____

October 18

Did you know that the water in the pipes in your home is regulated by pressure? The pressure in the pipes must be higher than the air pressure around them, so when the faucet is turned on, the water will flow, and-it will stop flowing when you turn the faucet off. This concept makes me think of GOD's Love is like the water in the pipes, and the heart is like the faucet that regulates GOD's Love flow. You see, GOD's Love is inside each of us. **John 4:7-8.** GOD's desire is for our love faucet to be open all the time to share HIS LOVE, but sometimes fear and anxiety turn our heart faucet off, and GOD's Love stops flowing. Don't let Satan inject fear and anxiety into your heart. Let GOD's Love flow through you today.

✝

Key Bible Verse

John 4:7-8 – "When a Samaritan woman came to draw water, Jesus said to her, "Will you give me a drink?" (His disciples had gone into the town to buy food.)"

Prayers & Notes

_____

_____

_____

_____

A Blessing from Yesterday _____

Something I am Thankful for Today _____

October 19

In 2016, Elon Musk, a wealthy American entrepreneur and founder of SpaceX, predicted his spaceship would take 100 people to the planet Mars by 2024. Hundreds of people put their names on a list to go, even though the trip would take seven months and is currently a one-way ticket. Now, that's a either a bold commitment or just crazy, huh? The only list I want my name on is the one in the Book of Life mentioned in **Revelation 20:15**. That is also a one-way trip, but it's to Heaven where we get to spend eternity with our HEAVENLY FATHER in paradise. Make a commitment to JESUS today, and let's help others who don't know him have the same opportunity. Tell others about HIM today!

✝

Key Bible Verse

Revelation 20:15 – "Anyone whose name was not found written in the book of life was thrown into the lake of fire."

Prayers & Notes

_____

_____

_____

_____

A Blessing from Yesterday _____

Something I am Thankful for Today _____

Patrick E. Moore

October 20

While visiting a friend's farm home, I was admiring the beautiful wooden pine floor throughout the house. It was made from large, old, seasoned pine timber sawn into beautiful new planks at an old, Amish sawmill. Each plank was a different width with worm holes and marks that let you know it was old and gave the floor character and beauty at the same time. Each plank had been cut and installed to fit perfectly. This morning, that floor reminded me of the Christian body that makes up the church. Each of us is different. Some are seasoned like those pine timbers, but we have all been made new in Christ just like those new planks. The Apostle Paul, in **Ephesians 4:16**, says if we each do our job and live-in love, the body of CHRIST that makes up the Church will fit together perfectly. Let's each do our job today in CHRIST.

Key Bible Verse

Ephesians 4:16 – "From him the whole body, joined and held together by every supporting ligament, grows and builds itself up in love, as each part does its work."

Prayers & Notes

_____

_____

_____

_____

A Blessing from Yesterday _____

Something I am Thankful for Today _____

October 21

I saw a video on Facebook of someone carefully tip toeing on steps made from metal rods anchored into the side of a rock cliff. The caption under the picture was "sometimes you need to step outside your comfort zone." Wow, I'll say. Stepping out of your comfort zone is a powerful way to grow personally, overcome fears, and gain self-esteem. The same is true in our spiritual lives. Teaching my first Sunday school class, going on my first mission trip, baptizing a dying friend in his bathtub and sharing my testimony in front of the church were all outside my comfort zone, but GOD was with me and my faith grew because of these experiences. **2 Timothy 1:7** says, "For GOD has not given us a spirit of fear and timidity, but of power, love and self-discipline. Step out in faith today!

Key Bible Verse

2 Timothy 1:7 – "For the Spirit God gave us does not make us timid, but gives us power, love and self-discipline."

Prayers & Notes

_____

_____

_____

_____

A Blessing from Yesterday _____

Something I am Thankful for Today _____

Patrick E. Moore

October 22

Last night, while waiting for our church choir practice to begin, I was chatting with a good friend about the frustration of trying to sing with a mask and social distance seating. I told her I would be soooo glad when things got back to normal. With a smile she replied, "Normal is a setting on a washing machine," and I laughed. Then I started thinking about what normal is. In the secular world, nothing is normal, because the world is always changing, right? But, in our spiritual life, there is a normal. It is Holiness, and GOD commands HIS followers to aspire to HIS standard. "Command" is not a suggestion, but "aspire" indicates we can never reach perfection. **Leviticus 20:7**. The apostle Peter explains what Holiness is in **1 Peter 1:13-15**. It is what we do. Aspire for GOD's normal this day and always!

Key Bible Verse

1 Peter 1:15 – "But just as he who called you is holy, so be holy in all you do"

Prayers & Notes

_____

_____

_____

_____

A Blessing from Yesterday _____

Something I am Thankful for Today _____

October 23

My Grandmother, Mimmaw, loved playing cards, especially bridge or canasta. Sometimes I would play with the cards and stack them to try to build a house, but I never had much luck. I read the Guinness world record for stacking cards is over 25 feet which seems impossible. As an adult, I learned that "building a house of cards" also meant something else. Sometimes people, through deceit or lies, build a life or business that will eventually come tumbling down like a house of cards. Often, peer pressure, pride or ego opens the door for Satan to convince us to tell lies in the first place. We are all guilty at some level, right? Not telling the truth was also a problem in JESUS' day. In **John 8:31-32**, JESUS tells the people to abide in HIS WORD, "then you will know the truth and the truth will set you free." Let's abide in HIS WORD today so we can be set free!

Key Bible Verse

John 8:31-32 – "To the Jews who had believed him, Jesus said, "If you hold to my teaching, you are really my disciples. Then you will know the truth, and the truth will set you free.""

Prayers & Notes

_____

_____

_____

A Blessing from Yesterday _____

Something I am Thankful for Today _____

Patrick E. Moore

October 24

This morning as I opened the door to my back porch, it dawned on me that we open and shut doors all day long in our daily lives. Most of these doors are open or unlocked, but it could be hundreds each day. By the way, the door industry is worth $140 billion. WOW. I then I remembered doors are mentioned a lot in our Bible – 189 times, by one count. There are many passages you would recognize, but the one that stands out to me is **John 10:9**. JESUS said, "I am the door, if anyone enters by me, he will be saved and will go in and out and find pasture." If you don't know JESUS, seek HIM today. HIS door is always open. Try and remember to thank JESUS every time you go through a door today. Remember, HIS door will never close on you!

✝

Key Bible Verse

John 10:9 – "I am the gate; whoever enters through me will be saved. They will come in and go out and find pasture."

Prayers & Notes

_____

_____

_____

_____

A Blessing from Yesterday _____

Something I am Thankful for Today _____

October 25

As I walked the dog last night, it was cold and damp with the wet autumn-colored leaves clumped in the driveway. I remembered just five days ago it was 80 degrees and sunny. Wow, seasons seem to change overnight, huh? It reminds me that Christian life also has changing seasons we must deal with. There could be a Dry season, when we seem more distant from GOD, or a Waiting season, when GOD may be pruning us for something, or maybe we are in a stressful Grinding or Busy season, Finally, maybe we are going through the Trial or Tribulation season, which is very painful. Remember **Ecclesiastes 3:1** says, "there is a season for everything!" Stay faithful. A happy season is just around the corner. Trust HIM Today!

✝

Key Bible Verse

Ecclesiastes 3:1 – "There is a time for everything, and a season for every activity under the heavens."

Prayers & Notes

_____

_____

_____

_____

A Blessing from Yesterday _____

Something I am Thankful for Today _____

October 26

Sometimes when GOD calls us to do something scary or uncomfortable, we ignore HIM or even run from the calling. Our reaction may not be from fear but because we know GOD will probably change some things in our lives we don't want changed. It happened to Jonah of whale fame in the Bible. He fled GOD's calling to preach in Nineveh not because of fear, but because he hated them as enemies and he didn't want GOD to save them. He wanted his hate to continue. After GOD saved Jonah, he did what GOD asked, and Nineveh was saved. Here is a question for us today. Is there something in your life GOD is calling you to do today? Maybe HE is calling you to forgive a loved one, or pray for an enemy, or give up something in your life that is hindering your own witness. Don't flee. Trust HIM. HE has a plan! **Proverbs 3:5-6.**

Key Bible Verse

Proverbs 3:5-6 – "Trust in the LORD with all your heart and lean not on your own understanding; in all your ways submit to him, and he will make your paths straight."

Prayers & Notes

_____

_____

_____

_____

A Blessing from Yesterday _____

Something I am Thankful for Today _____

October 27

This morning, I am thinking about my heritage and those who came before me. Thanks to my sister Carole who is our family's genealogy expert, we know many of their names and history. As a veteran and patriotic sort, I was proud to learn about those who have fought on my behalf since the Revolutionary War. I am also proud and thankful that we have a heritage of God-fearing people who fought some spiritual battles along the way so I wouldn't have to. How do I know? Because the LORD has blessed us, and it says in **Deuteronomy 7:9** our LORD is the "faithful GOD, keeping his covenant of love to a thousand generations of those who love him and keep his commandments." It's now our job to keep it going. Amen?

✝

Key Bible Verse

Deuteronomy 7:9 – "Know therefore that the LORD your God is God; he is the faithful God, keeping his covenant of love to a thousand generations of those who love him and keep his commandments."

Prayers & Notes

_____

_____

_____

_____

A Blessing from Yesterday _____

Something I am Thankful for Today _____

300   Patrick E. Moore

October 28

I ran across a Charles Spurgeon quote yesterday that caught my mind's eye. One of the greatest preachers of all time, Spurgeon was born and raised in England and died in 1892. He said, "The Lord's servants cannot serve HIM in their own strength, for they cannot even live unless HIS Grace abounds toward them." Wow, that is so true. Yes, we are called to serve our Heavenly FATHER, but we need to humbly recognize it's in GOD's strength that we do it. The Apostle Paul says this in **Philippians 2:13:** "for it is GOD who works in you to will and to act in order to fulfill HIS good purpose." Today is a great day for us to thank our Heavenly FATHER for HIS son JESUS who gives us, first, Grace from sin and second, Strength to serve HIM daily. Amen.

Key Bible Verse

Philippians 2:13 – "for it is God who works in you to will and to act in order to fulfill his good purpose."

Prayers & Notes

_____

_____

_____

_____

A Blessing from Yesterday _____

Something I am Thankful for Today _____

October 29

Boy, does our country need a Revival. We are extremely polarized as a nation politically, morally, ethically and spiritually, and we need our land to be healed. Christian, be clear. This is not about a candidate, a political party, a government or any law. It's about the heart. The only solution is a renewal of our hearts, minds and souls back to the things of CHRIST. That is what a revival is. The prophet Ezra wrote in **2 Chronicles 7:14,** "if my people, who are called by my name, will humble themselves and pray and seek my face and turn from their wicked ways, then I will hear from heaven, and I will forgive their sin and will heal their land." Please pray for healing.

Key Bible Verse

2 Chronicles 7:14 – "If my people, who are called by my name, will humble themselves and pray and seek my face and turn from their wicked ways, then I will hear from heaven, and I will forgive their sin and will heal their land."

Prayers & Notes

_____

_____

_____

_____

A Blessing from Yesterday _____

Something I am Thankful for Today _____

Patrick E. Moore

October 30

Ever receive a letter or package in your mailbox box that you didn't want or ask for? Did you write "return to sender" on that parcel and put it back in the mailbox? Now imagine, Satan attacks you or your family with lies, sickness, fear, worry or worse. Remember GOD is not the sender of bad things that happen. That is Satan. **Ephesians 6:12** says we are fighting evil, spiritual forces. It's sort of like that package that you got by the mistake in the mailbox. You didn't want it, deserve or need it, but maybe you don't know what to do now. We need faith to believe we can "return it to sender." The Bible says in **James 4:7** we should "submit ourselves to GOD. Resist the devil and he will flee from you." Speak...no, shout to the evil one when fear or sickness comes. Tell him he has no authority in a child of GOD, in the name of JESUS. Return that evil to the sender!

Key Bible Verse

James 4:7 – "Submit yourselves, then, to God. Resist the devil, and he will flee from you."

Prayers & Notes

_____

_____

_____

_____

A Blessing from Yesterday _____

Something I am Thankful for Today _____

October 31

I saw a quote yesterday that I liked, "you cannot control the direction of the wind, but you can adjust your sails." That quote or a version of it goes back to the early to mid 1800's and has been used in churches, prayer books, playwrights, motivational books and even under a picture of Dolly Parton at Dollywood where I saw it. To me, this strikes at the heart of our attitudes when things don't go right in life and to the choices we make to adjust and deal with change I know from experience that I can adjust better when I let GOD be a part of the equation. **Proverbs 3:5-6** says, "Trust in the LORD with all your heart and lean not on your own understanding; in all your ways submit to him, and he will make your paths straight." Don't let the winds of life blow you off GOD's direction for your life. Keep HIM nearby.

Key Bible Verse

Proverbs 3:5-6 – "Trust in the LORD with all your heart and lean not on your own understanding; in all your ways submit to him, and he will make your paths straight"

Prayers & Notes

_____

_____

_____

A Blessing from Yesterday _____

Something I am Thankful for Today _____

Patrick E. Moore

November 1

This morning, I am sitting in a rocking chair on a porch overlooking the stunning fall colors of the Great Smoky Mountains. The air is cool with a touch of hazy fog hovering over the top of the trees. We are concluding a two-day trip to Dollywood with two of our grandsons. While the boys logged over 24,000 steps running between rides, Karen and I enjoyed sitting and listening to the great music of the park. My favorite group, The Kingdom Heirs, are a southern gospel quartet that have been singing at Dollywood for over 30 years. Their song "I'll never get over the Blood I am under" says it all in the title of the song, but the line "I'll never wonder where I will spend eternity" is one to rejoice over if you know JESUS CHRIST. **Hebrews 10:19**. May we never get over the blood we are under.

Key Bible Verse

Hebrews 10:19 – "Therefore, brothers and sisters, since we have confidence to enter the Most Holy Place by the blood of Jesus,"

Prayers & Notes

_____

_____

_____

_____

A Blessing from Yesterday _____

Something I am Thankful for Today _____

November 2

We don't need to read Psychology Today to realize humans have an intense need to be loved and nurtured. All we need to do is to watch a newborn baby and see the most basic emotions in the baby's Mother. Since GOD is Love and because we were created in GOD's image, we must have inherited emotion from GOD. Did you know that GOD has "Hesed" love for us? Hesed love is only mentioned in the Old Testament, and it describes a love that only GOD can have for us. It is a merciful, unconditional, unfathomable and loyal love that comes from the covenant GOD made with Abraham and his descendants. Yes, we all need love, and we can be confident in the love our Heavenly FATHER has for us now and forevermore. **Deuteronomy 4:31**. Do you know HIM? Feel HIS love today!

Key Bible Verse

Deuteronomy 4:31 – "For the LORD your God is a merciful God; he will not abandon or destroy you or forget the covenant with your ancestors, which he confirmed to them by oath."

Prayers & Notes

_____

_____

_____

A Blessing from Yesterday _____

Something I am Thankful for Today _____

306   Patrick E. Moore

November 3

Yes, today is Election Day in America and yes, I think we have an obligation to vote our conscience for who we think could lead our great country for the next four years. My prayer is that we, the people, will act with civility and respect towards each other regardless of the outcome. There is another vote that is more important than this political election; it is the vote we make to elect JESUS as our LORD and SAVIOR. The ramifications are greater than any four-year term; they are for eternity. I am proud to vote for JESUS today. Remember, "but for me and my house, we will serve the LORD" (**Joshua 24:15**. I hope you have already cast your vote for JESUS, but if not, this would be a great day to cast that vote as well.

✝

Key Bible Verse

Joshua 24:15 – "But if serving the LORD seems undesirable to you, then choose for yourselves this day whom you will serve, whether the gods your ancestors served beyond the Euphrates, or the gods of the Amorites, in whose land you are living. But as for me and my household, we will serve the LORD."

Prayers & Notes

_____

_____

_____

_____

A Blessing from Yesterday _____

Something I am Thankful for Today _____

No Mountain Too High

November 4

You may be waking up disappointed this morning because the election didn't go the way you wanted and hoped. It's ok to be disappointed but it can be painful. Remember, disappointment is an emotion and not a terminal illness, and we must be careful that it doesn't become a seed of bitterness and hate, which then becomes sin. So, start by expressing your feelings of pain and disappointment to GOD...out loud. Yes, your Heavenly FATHER is the perfect listener for any painful thing. He won't judge you or argue with you; will just listen. **Philippians 4:6-7** is a great passage to read when you are disappointed. It ends with, "and the peace of GOD which transcends all understanding, will guard your hearts and minds in CHRIST JESUS." Let GOD have your disappointment, and HE will give you peace.

Key Bible Verse

Philippians 4:6-7 – "Do not be anxious about anything, but in every situation, by prayer and petition, with thanksgiving, present your requests to God. And the peace of God, which transcends all understanding, will guard your hearts and your minds in Christ Jesus."

Prayers & Notes

_____

_____

_____

A Blessing from Yesterday _____

Something I am Thankful for Today _____

Patrick E. Moore

November 5

The modern-day shepherd in the Middle East knows each of his sheep by name. They will come individually when they are called, even among a herd of hundreds, because they recognize the voice of their shepherd. The shepherd's job is to lead the sheep to greener pastures, to water, and to protect them. The people of JESUS' time knew this when HE spoke about being their Shepherd in the New Testament (**John 10:7-9**). They didn't really understand it then, but we should understand it now. Do you know the GOOD Shepherd? HIS name is JESUS, and HE is calling us to HIM. Listen for HIS voice and HE will lead you to greener pastures.

✝

Key Bible Verse

John 10:7-9 – Therefore Jesus said again, "Very truly I tell you, I am the gate for the sheep. All who have come before me are thieves and robbers, but the sheep have not listened to them. I am the gate; whoever enters through me will be saved. They will come in and go out and find pasture.

Prayers & Notes

_____

_____

_____

_____

A Blessing from Yesterday _____

Something I am Thankful for Today _____

November 6

The Greek word "symphonia" means "to sound together, accordant, harmonious, concert of instruments, music" and is the origin of the word symphony. I truly love Christian music, and it is a big part of my worship every day. If you have ever heard a symphony warming up, it sounds like chaos before they start following the conductor simultaneously, and then we hear a harmonious sound. If you think about our world today, it is in chaos. We need to turn our eyes, hearts, praise and worship to GOD, who is the Supreme Conductor of our lives. HE is the author of all music and is writing a symphony amid the chaos. Christians everywhere need to turn our voices of praise towards GOD today so the rest of the world can enjoy the music OF HIS Love. Amen? **Ephesians 5:19-21**

Key Bible Verse

Ephesians 5:19-21 – speaking to one another with psalms, hymns, and songs from the Spirit. Sing and make music from your heart to the Lord, always giving thanks to God the Father for everything, in the name of our Lord Jesus Christ.

Prayers & Notes

_____

_____

_____

_____

A Blessing from Yesterday _____

Something I am Thankful for Today _____

Patrick E. Moore

November 7

We have all heard the statement "nothing lasts forever," right? If you are talking about earthly things, that is correct. It's true for every physical thing you can think of including our own health and mortality. It's also true in politics, music, jobs, sports, our money and anything else you can think of...with one exception. It's our eternal salvation that comes through the Grace of CHRIST JESUS if we have accepted HIM. **Isaiah 51:6**. Yes, while everything else fades away, our salvation is forever. Next time you hear that statement, you can note the one exception. Will you? Thank HIM today!

Key Bible Verse

Isaiah 51:6 – "Lift up your eyes to the heavens, look at the earth beneath; the heavens will vanish like smoke, the earth will wear out like a garment and its inhabitants die like flies. But my salvation will last forever, my righteousness will never fail.'

Prayers & Notes

_____

_____

_____

_____

_____

A Blessing from Yesterday _____

Something I am Thankful for Today _____

No Mountain Too High

November 8

Have you ever thought about the number of decisions we make in a day? Research says it could be a mind boggling 35,000 per day. Whaaattt?! Thank goodness most of those decisions are involuntary, automatic, or reflexive. The studies of neuroscience say the brain makes a decision up to ten seconds before the rest of the body reacts. Fascinating, huh? Decisions come from choices. The conscience choices we make every day will shape our destiny in life on this earth, but the choices we make around GOD will affect our Eternal destiny. Make as many decisions as you can each day with GOD in mind, and let HIM transform you for the purpose HE has intended for your life. **Romans 12:2**. Be Blessed.

Key Bible Verse

Romans 12:2 – "Do not conform to the pattern of this world but be transformed by the renewing of your mind. Then you will be able to test and approve what God's will is—his good, pleasing and perfect will."

Prayers & Notes

_____

_____

_____

_____

A Blessing from Yesterday _____

Something I am Thankful for Today _____

Patrick E. Moore

November 9

GOD sent HIS SON JESUS as a gift to all of humanity, but to receive it, you must accept it. My prayer is that you have. When we receive the gift of JESUS, we all receive a measure of Faith. **Romans 12:3**. With GOD's help and our efforts, our Faith will grow. However, we need to be clear that Faith won't take away the problems of life, or the pain that comes with them. However, it will give us the ability to handle the pain. Using an analogy of weather, Faith won't take away the storms of life, but it will keep you calm in the midst of them. Rejoice in HIM today!

Key Bible Verse

Romans 12:3 – "For by the grace given me I say to every one of you: Do not think of yourself more highly than you ought, but rather think of yourself with sober judgment, in accordance with the faith God has distributed to each of you."

Prayers & Notes

_____

_____

_____

_____

_____

A Blessing from Yesterday _____

Something I am Thankful for Today _____

November 10

Every organ of our body is an amazing part of GOD's creation, but I am partial to the eyes and I'm so thankful that mine are healthy. My Mother was legally blind for the last 15 years of her life because of optic nerve disease, but she still was an organ donor of the healthy part of her eyes. Because of her gift, two blind recipients were able to see again. That was a legacy blessing. The Bible says eyes are like windows to our hearts (**Matthew 6:22-24**). You see, our eyes are like a camera lens that, when open, allows light in. If we keep our eyes focused on the things of GOD, which are love and all things good, then GOD's light will shine and fill our souls. If we turn our eyes away from GOD, we will have darkness, and evil will replace the good in our souls. Keep your eyes on GOD today, so your heart and soul will be filled with HIS light.

Key Bible Verse

Matthew 6:22 – "The eye is the lamp of the body. If your eyes are healthy, your whole body will be full of light. But if your eyes are unhealthy, your whole body will be full of darkness. If then the light within you is darkness, how great is that darkness!"

Prayers & Notes

_____

_____

_____

A Blessing from Yesterday _____

Something I am Thankful for Today _____

Patrick E. Moore

November 11

We have some beautiful Maple trees in our front yard that we planted over twenty years ago. Their display of stunning colors has not disappointed us as autumn is now giving way to Winter. It rained last night, so many of the leaves fell and left a blanket of GOD's handiwork in the yard. I love the autumn weather and colors, but it's time for a transition. It's like life. We go through seasons of life that give way to the next season. This year has been a difficult season for all of us, but for Christians, GOD promises us HE will never leave or forsake us, so we shouldn't be dismayed. **Deuteronomy 31:8**. Do you know HIM? Thank HIM that seasons are not forever, but HE is!

✝

Key Bible Verse

Deuteronomy 31:8 – "The LORD himself goes before you and will be with you; he will never leave you nor forsake you. Do not be afraid; do not be discouraged."

Prayers & Notes

_____

_____

_____

_____

_____

A Blessing from Yesterday _____

Something I am Thankful for Today _____

November 12

The Blessings of life are not just gifts like the ones we might put on lay away before Christmas. No, the ultimate Blessing GOD gives to all who have Faith and accept HIM as LORD and SAVIOR is the gift of Eternal salvation. **Romans 6:23**. The greater our Faith is in GOD, the greater will be the additional Blessings of kindness, good health, loving spirit, patience and forgiveness which can lead to even more earthly and physical blessings. Sometimes we get confused about our earthly blessings and think they only come from our good works, but that is false. The Blessings in our lives will increase if our Faith grows and we glorify GOD more with the gifts HE gives us. Don't let your Blessings be put on layaway. Glorify GOD daily!

Key Bible Verse

Romans 6:23 – "For the wages of sin is death, but the gift of God is eternal life in Christ Jesus our Lord."

Prayers & Notes

_____

_____

_____

_____

_____

A Blessing from Yesterday _____

Something I am Thankful for Today _____

Patrick E. Moore

November 13

Did you know that anchors have been used with boats since the Bronze Age which was over 5000 years ago? Whether it was a large rock with a hole in it, a bag of rocks, or a traditional iron anchor, boats, and now ships need something to keep the boat steady during storms or rough seas. Thus, we have the anchor. Speaking of stormy times, this year has been a non-stop storm, huh? Since this pandemic started, our minds have been flooded with "what if" scenarios. Our thoughts start as doubt, then move to fear and then lead to torment. Christians, how do we stop them? The first thing is to realize "what if" questions don't come from GOD; they are from Satan. Next, we need to drop the anchor of GOD's WORD into the storm. It will take away the doubt, fear and torment. **Hebrews 6:19.** Drop GOD's anchor into your storm today!

✝

Key Bible Verse

Hebrews 6:19 – "We have this hope as an anchor for the soul, firm and secure. It enters the inner sanctuary behind the curtain,"

Prayers & Notes

_____

_____

_____

_____

A Blessing from Yesterday _____

Something I am Thankful for Today _____

November 14

Do you ever use the mile markers on the interstate when you're driving? They can come in very handy if you need road assistance or you're trying to determine how far you are from your exit or the state line. That reminds me there are also spiritual mile markers on the journey through life. However, spiritual mile markers usually mark the place we have been or have come from. It usually reminds us of a significant place or time where God protected us, used us, or guided us. Even though some of the mile markers represent unhappy events, GOD has used them to keep me on my journey to my eternal resting place. Review your spiritual mile markers to see where you have been and how far you have come with GOD's Grace. **Jeremiah 31:21**

Key Bible Verse

Jeremiah 31:21 - "Set up road signs; put up guideposts. Take note of the highway, the road that you take. Return, Virgin Israel, return to your towns."

Prayers & Notes

_____

_____

_____

_____

_____

A Blessing from Yesterday _____

Something I am Thankful for Today _____

Patrick E. Moore

November 15

One of the greatest movies of all time was "It's a Wonderful Life" with Jimmy Stewart, and surprisingly Hollywood scripted a subtle Christian message by casting a guardian angel to save Jimmy Stewart's life. Good for Hollywood. By the way, do you believe in angels? I sure do. There are over 250 references of two angels in the Bible. In **Hebrews 13:2**, the Apostle Paul says, "Do not forget to entertain strangers, for by so doing, some have unwittingly entertained angels." There are numerous incidences of GOD sending angels to HIS people to give us messages, to protect us, to serve us, to execute judgment against GOD's enemies (as told in **2 Kings 19:35**), or to give Praise and Worship to GOD. It makes sense that the more we read GOD's WORD, Worship and Pray to allow our Faith to grow, the busier GOD's Angels would be on earth. Let's get busy!

✝

Key Bible Verse

Hebrews 13:2 – "Do not forget to show hospitality to strangers, for by so doing some people have shown hospitality to angels without knowing it."

Prayers & Notes

_____

_____

_____

_____

A Blessing from Yesterday _____

Something I am Thankful for Today _____

November 16

With our country and world in turmoil, we must turn to Prayer and Love until GOD's Glory returns. The same turmoil invades our life with our own broken relationships and our enemies. The same answer is needed, Prayer and Love. The Apostle Paul reminds us in **Romans 8:38** "that nothing can separate us from GOD's Love," and Heaven knows we don't deserve it. Our culture, led by evil influence, wants to separate us from each other, to hate our enemies, to turn our back on those who have hurt us, but GOD tells us and shows us that the answer is Love. Aren't you thankful GOD didn't stop loving us when we didn't deserve it? It's time for us to Love like JESUS loved, speak like JESUS spoke and walked like JESUS walked. Let the revival in your heart begin today!

✝

Key Bible Verse

Romans 8:38 – "For I am convinced that neither death nor life, neither angels nor demons, neither the present nor the future, nor any powers,"

Prayers & Notes

_____

_____

_____

_____

A Blessing from Yesterday _____

Something I am Thankful for Today _____

Patrick E. Moore

November 17

Even though I was not the brightest bulb in the chandelier during English classes, I have always paid great attention to the words people use in what they say and write. Often times, people say or write contrasting words in their sentences to highlight their differences. That's called a juxtaposition. The Bible is full of juxtapositions. I was reminded of that as I read **Ephesians 2:1-5** this morning. Paraphrasing, it says we are dead in sin or alive with CHRIST. Contrasting thoughts, right? What does dead mean? It means anything that JESUS wasn't. It can mean physical, emotional or spiritual death, i.e., sickness, depression or fear, or without faith. Alive in CHRIST is everything JESUS was, which means we can be healthy, joyful, at peace and Faithful to GOD's Glory. Worship HIM, and be Alive in CHRIST TODAY!

Key Bible Verse

Ephesians 2:4-5 – "But because of his great love for us, God, who is rich in mercy, made us alive with Christ even when we were dead in transgressions—it is by grace you have been saved."

Prayers & Notes

_____

_____

_____

_____

A Blessing from Yesterday _____

Something I am Thankful for Today _____

November 18

If you have grandkids, like I do, you have probably heard of Buzz Light-year, one of the hero characters in the kid's movie "Toy Story." His slogan was, "To infinity and beyond!" "Toy Story" was a great movie, and interestingly, Tim Allen did the voice over for Buzz. Was does infinity mean? Webster's says it mean "unlimited extent of time, space or quantity: boundless." In a recent study of Matthew and JESUS' crucifixion, the word infinity was used to describe JESUS, which really convicted me. Think about it. JESUS took all of the pain and suffering for of the sins of all mankind for all time to the cross! Friend, that includes you and me. Now that is the infinity nature of GOD as stated in **Psalms 19:1**. Thank GOD today for the infinite nature of HIS son JESUS. Amen?

Key Bible Verse

Psalms 19:1 – "The heavens declare the glory of God; the skies proclaim the work of his hands."

Prayers & Notes

_____

_____

_____

_____

A Blessing from Yesterday _____

Something I am Thankful for Today _____

November 19

This morning, while reading "A Small Book of Prayers for Great Big Power," by Erica Diggs, I was reminded that GOD answers all of our prayers if we are praying with the complete faith and confidence that HIS work is already done. Then, we must persist in our prayers until we see the earthly manifestation of GOD's answers. Why persist? GOD could be teaching us something with the waiting, or angels may be battling demons along the way and our persistent prayers give the angels power. This happened to Daniel, as described in Daniel 9, when it took the angel Gabriel twenty-one days to deliver GOD's answer to Daniel's prayers. Thank goodness for Daniel's persistence and for ours when we pray. GOD promised our prayers will not return void (**Isaiah 55:11**). Pray with Trust and Faith today!

✝

Key Bible Verse

Isaiah 55:11 – "so is my word that goes out from my mouth: It will not return to me empty but will accomplish what I desire and achieve the purpose for which I sent it."

Prayers & Notes

_____

_____

_____

_____

A Blessing from Yesterday _____

Something I am Thankful for Today _____

November 20

If you grew up in the '60's, you probably remember the song "Wishin' and Hopin'" by Dusty Springfield. It was a number one hit on the pop charts in America. It is a love song about a woman trying to get her man, but wishin' and hopin' won't do it. There is a bit of theology in that song when it comes to our prayer life. You see, hope is "a feeling of expectation and desire for a certain thing to happen." Hope is a good thing, but like the song says, you won't get your man's attention, (in this case, JESUS) with hope alone. We also need to add Faith, "complete trust and confidence in someone," to our prayer of hope to give it substance. I am talking about having Faith of what JESUS has already done on the cross for you us. Add Faith to your prayers and see what happens. **Mark 11:24**.

Key Bible Verse

Mark 11:24 – "Therefore I tell you, whatever you ask for in prayer, believe that you have received it, and it will be yours."

Prayers & Notes

_____

_____

_____

_____

_____

A Blessing from Yesterday _____

Something I am Thankful for Today _____

Patrick E. Moore

November 21

Contamination is when something is made impure through polluting or poisoning. One example is food poisoning, and if you have ever experienced that, you know how sick it can make you until your body gets rid of the contamination. That can also happen to one's Spiritual Life. Sometimes Faith gets contaminated by fear, worry, anger, or jealousy, and it can make your Spirit sick. These are attacks by Satan, and we must recognize the symptoms. **2 Timothy 1:7** says, "For the Spirit God gave us does not make us timid, but gives us power, love and self-discipline," and that is not fear. Claim GOD's Truth today, and make your Faith well again!

Key Bible Verse

2 Timothy 1:7 – "For the Spirit God gave us does not make us timid, but gives us power, love and self-discipline."

Prayers & Notes

_____

_____

_____

_____

_____

_____

A Blessing from Yesterday _____

Something I am Thankful for Today _____

No Mountain Too High

November 22

The world eagerly awaits the release of a vaccine for the current pandemic in hopes it will cure this physical disease, Covid-19. I can remember taking a polio vaccine as a boy, and thankfully that disease was eradicated in the U.S. in 1979. We also are susceptible to Spiritual diseases. One that is flourishing now is the spirit of unbelief which causes a multitude of symptoms such as anger, anxiety, hate, insecurity, jealously, and, most prevalent, fear. I heard or read a great quote this week that said, "the only cure for unbelief is Belief." You see, fear doesn't stop you from dying, it stops you from living. Therefore, seek GOD's WORD through prayer to cure your unbelief. **Mark 9:23-24.** Start today!

Key Bible Verse

Mark 9:23-24 - "'If you can'?" said Jesus. "Everything is possible for one who believes." Immediately the boy's father exclaimed, "I do believe; help me overcome my unbelief!"

Prayers & Notes

_____

_____

_____

_____

A Blessing from Yesterday _____

Something I am Thankful for Today _____

Patrick E. Moore

November 23

This past weekend we visited family in Waynesville N.C. in the foothills of the Smoky Mountains. The mountains reminded me of the Boy Scout trip my brother and I made to Philmont, New Mexico, as 15-year-olds. The camp was in the foothills of the Cimarron Mountain Range, and our adventure included a four-day hike to the peak of a 12,441 ft. mountain called "Old Baldy. "That mountaintop experience was unforgettable. In **Luke 9:23-37**, the apostles Peter, John and James had an unforgettable mountain experience with JESUS during HIS Transformation into dazzling Glory. It wouldn't have been the same if the apostles had watched from the foothills. They were changed by climbing that mountain. Our spiritual journey is a climb to the mountaintop to be with JESUS. Don't stop climbing. I know it can be hard, but the mountaintop experience will be eternal.

✝

Key Bible Verse

Luke 9:28-30 — "About eight days after Jesus said this, he took Peter, John and James with him and went up onto a mountain to pray. As he was praying, the appearance of his face changed, and his clothes became as bright as a flash of lightning. Two men, Moses and Elijah, appeared in glorious splendor, talking with Jesus. "

Prayers & Notes

_____

_____

_____

A Blessing from Yesterday _____

Something I am Thankful for Today _____

No Mountain Too High

November 24

While listening to an audio book while driving Sunday, I heard this phrase, "kindness was just an inch outside her reach." The author was describing a character's lack of kindness to most people, and it dawned on me that many words could be interchangeable with "kindness" to describe any of us. For example, trust, belief, faith, love, peace, and hope might be "just an inch outside our reach" sometimes when things get tough. Here is the Good News. GOD's Love for us is always within reach, but you must let HIM in. It is written, "And behold, I am with you always, to the end of the age." **Matthew 28:20**. Bless HIM TODAY.

Key Bible Verse

Matthew 28:20 – "and teaching them to obey everything I have commanded you. And surely I am with you always, to the very end of the age."

Prayers & Notes

_____

_____

_____

_____

_____

_____

A Blessing from Yesterday _____

Something I am Thankful for Today _____

Patrick E. Moore

November 25

I am old enough to remember the old western TV shows we watched on our black and white TV. I loved to watch Roy Rogers, Gene Autry, The Lone Ranger, and many more. They all had quick triggers, which is an old gunslinger term. Trigger is also a verb that means to cause an event or situation to happen or exist. It happens frequently with our emotions or feelings. This morning while reading "A Small Book of Prayers for Great Big Power," by Erica Diggs, I noted the sentence, "Satan loves to trigger or ignite people into unbelief by keeping them in their feelings and emotions and not in faith." Remember, if it's not of faith, it is a sin (**Romans 14:23**). Pray that GOD will protect you from Satan's attacks today!

✝

Key Bible Verse

Romans 14:23 – "But whoever has doubts is condemned if they eat, because their eating is not from faith; and everything that does not come from faith is sin."

Prayers & Notes

_____

_____

_____

_____

A Blessing from Yesterday _____

Something I am Thankful for Today _____

No Mountain Too High   329

November 26

Our physical balance, including our spatial orientation, allows the body to judge where it is in space; the scientific word is proprioception. For example, it allows us to balance on one foot and to navigate steps without looking down at them. As we get older, this sense deteriorates, and we might find ourselves stumbling on steps or uneven surfaces. What about balance in our Spiritual lives as Christians? We should be balanced in our daily lives, staying levelheaded, not overly dogmatic and respectful of other beliefs even when they are not our own, but we should be totally unbalanced in our love for CHRIST. In **Luke 10:27**, JESUS says "You shall love the Lord your God with all your heart and with all your soul and with all your strength and with all your mind, and your neighbor as yourself." Express your love for JESUS today.

Key Bible Verse

Luke 10:27 – "He answered, "'Love the Lord your God with all your heart and with all your soul and with all your strength and with all your mind'; and 'Love your neighbor as yourself.'"

Prayers & Notes

_____

_____

_____

_____

A Blessing from Yesterday _____

Something I am Thankful for Today _____

Patrick E. Moore

November 27

You have probably heard the term "red letter day" which refers to any day that is pleasantly memorable or noteworthy. It comes from the Roman dynasty, around 500 BC, when important days were written in red ink on the calendar. Another red-letter tradition started in 1901 when the first Bible was printed with red letters, signifying the words JESUS spoke. You will find this in most Bibles today in Matthew, Mark, Luke and John. For some reason, I opened the book of Luke and started reading only the red letters. GOD's awesome character is revealed with those words. Try it for yourself. I stopped reading when I got to **Luke 6:43-44** when JESUS said, "a tree will be known for its fruit." What a simple but awesome message. What kind of fruit are we producing? May it be glorifying to GOD today.

Key Bible Verse

Luke 6:43-44 - "No good tree bears bad fruit, nor does a bad tree bear good fruit. Each tree is recognized by its own fruit. People do not pick figs from thorn bushes, or grapes from briers."

Prayers & Notes

_____

_____

_____

_____

A Blessing from Yesterday _____

Something I am Thankful for Today _____

November 28

My prayer walk was a little cool but still pleasant this autumn morning, but old man winter is forecasted to bring a sudden change with freezing temperatures and snow within 48 hours. Bbbrrrhhh, I am just not ready for the cold. You know, our life circumstances, especially our health, can change suddenly also, and we might not be ready for that those changes, either. The question is how do we prepare for changing seasons of health, mental or emotional issues? The principles of preparedness go back to Genesis and the story of Noah. GOD's WORD has answers exemplified in **Genesis 6:21** where GOD told Noah to gather food for later use. Then Noah worked on the ark GOD told him to build over 120 years before using. What principles should we learn from this example? Live upright, prepare our hearts and souls by reading GOD's WORD, pray daily and listen to God for guidance, and then be obedient. That will prepare us for anything. Praise Him today!

Key Bible Verse

Genesis 6:21 – "You are to take every kind of food that is to be eaten and store it away as food for you and for them."

Prayers & Notes

_____

_____

_____

A Blessing from Yesterday _____

Something I am Thankful for Today _____

Patrick E. Moore

November 29

We started pulling out Christmas decorations yesterday. Fortunately, my sweet wife has them organized in large plastic bins and labeled by room which makes it easier. My job is to set up the outside decorations the two trees up while Karen decorates the inside rooms and makes a Christmas wreath for the front door. Watching her work on that wreath reminded me of GOD's never-ending love because a wreath is a circle with no beginning or end. That is just like the love GOD has for us. **Lamentations 3:22-24.** As you put up your decorations this year, look for the symbolism to remind you the reason for the season, and that is to celebrate the birth of CHRIST.

Key Bible Verse

Lamentations 3:22-24 – "Because of the LORD's great love we are not consumed, for his compassions never fail. They are new every morning; great is your faithfulness. I say to myself, "The LORD is my portion: therefore I will wait for him.""

Prayers & Notes

_____

_____

_____

_____

A Blessing from Yesterday _____

Something I am Thankful for Today _____

No Mountain Too High

November 30

As I get older, the years seem to go by faster. Our third grandson turns 15 today, and it just doesn't seem possible. Yes, time is flying by. GOD has blessed us with two beautiful daughters and five wonderful grandchildren that I pray for each and every day. Karen and I have made mistakes as parents and grandparents, but we have always been united in our most important priorities. The first is to teach them about GOD and take them to church, in hopes they develop a habit of staying in a faith community. Next is to make sure they are loved unconditionally, just like GOD loves us. Read **Romans 3:23** to be reminded of how GOD loves us. Last is to help them develop confidence in themselves but also in their Faith that GOD will always be there for them, and the rest should take care of itself. Thank GOD for your family today!

Key Bible Verse

Romans 3:23 – "for all have sinned and fall short of the glory of God,"

Prayers & Notes

_____

_____

_____

_____

_____

A Blessing from Yesterday _____

Something I am Thankful for Today _____

Patrick E. Moore

December 1

If you have ever had a child or been around babies, you know they have a natural reflex to suck on any and everything that gets close to their mouths. Modern ultrasounds have shown babies in the womb with fingers in their mouths, helping them build their adaptive reflexes to survive in the world. That reflex allows them to get the milk they need to survive until they are old enough to eat solid food. That sucking reflex keeps babies calm, and along comes the pacifier industry that sells 15 million "pacies," "binkies," and "foo foo's" each year. But eventually solid food is needed, and the pacifier must come out. What does this have to do with the Bible? A lot. The Apostle Paul in **1 Corinthians 3:2** addressed the early Christians by saying He initially had given them a basic understanding of CHRIST (the reference to milk), but now it is time for them to go deeper in the doctrine of their faith (the reference to solid food). That may apply to us today in our Faith. Are we satisfied with basic knowledge and haven't gone deeper in GOD's word to get "solid food" to grow our Faith? Maybe it's time to "take the pacifier out" and get into HIS WORD.

Key Bible Verse

1 Corinthians 3:2 – "I gave you milk, not solid food, for you were not yet ready for it. Indeed, you are still not ready."

Prayers & Notes

_____

_____

A Blessing from Yesterday _____

Something I am Thankful for Today _____

December 2

I awoke this morning a few minutes before the alarm went off, and for some reason the lyrics "saved a wretch like me" popped into my head. These are lyrics from the famous hymn, "Amazing Grace." Why these lyrics? I guess GOD wanted me to understand and share what that means to you and me. Wretch(ed) means "miserable, ill, a person in a very unhappy or unfortunate state." It is you, me and everyone because of our sin nature. But, as the song says, if we know and have accepted CHRIST, we, the wretched, are saved and washed clean in the blood of JESUS, over...and over...and over again! Here is the important thing to know: it is not because of anything we have or have not done. Nope, it's only because of GOD's Grace. The Apostle Paul says it well in **Ephesians 2:8,** "it is the gift of GOD." On bended knees this morning, I thanked GOD for saving a wretch like me. Will you?

Key Bible Verse

Ephesians 2:8 – "For it is by grace you have been saved, through faith—and this is not from yourselves, it is the gift of God—"

Prayers & Notes

_____

_____

_____

_____

A Blessing from Yesterday _____

Something I am Thankful for Today _____

336   Patrick E. Moore

December 3

Being a really good listener is a great but rare quality. Do you know any good listeners? Are you one? I admit I haven't always been a good listener, but I am really trying hard to be better. You see, it's not that our ears don't work properly, it's that we tend to hear what we want to hear. Our pride, bias, prejudice, ambition, and our Faith seem to filter how we listen. That is why two separate people can hear the same news and interpret it completely differently. As Christians, we need to learn how to listen with our hearts and spirits. **Proverbs 2:2** says, "so train your heart to listen when I speak and open your spirit wide to expand your discernment, then pass it on to your sons and daughters." The revelation is if we listen with our hearts, then we will be better at speaking hope and love to others, and that my friends is how you change the world. Ask GOD to improve your listening today.

✝

Key Bible Verse

Proverbs 2:2 – "turning your ear to wisdom and applying your heart to understanding"

Prayers & Notes

_____

_____

_____

A Blessing from Yesterday _____

Something I am Thankful for Today _____

December 4

As we turned out the lights last night to go to bed, Karen said there must be a light on upstairs because she could see a glow. When I went upstairs, I noticed we didn't turn off the Christmas tree, and it was shining so bright and beautiful in the darkness. It reminded me that GOD's Light shines bright and beautiful in a dark and sinful world. You see, the world doesn't like the light because darkness is where sin originates and exists. Our job, as Christians, is to let GOD's light shine brightly through us. Let's be like a Christmas tree shining in the dark for others to see. During this Christmas season, every time you turn on the lights on your Christmas tree, remember the light of GOD that shines through you. **Matthew 5:16.**

Key Bible Verse

Matthew 5:16. – "In the same way, let your light shine before others, that they may see your good deeds and glorify your Father in heaven."

Prayers & Notes

_____

_____

_____

_____

_____

A Blessing from Yesterday _____

Something I am Thankful for Today _____

December 5

Nearly two years ago, I received a scary diagnosis, and I entered into a healing season in earnest with my good friend Erica Diggs. I wanted to share this because everyone is, has, or will go through his or her own season of healing, whether physical, emotional, or spiritual. Erica started teaching me about GOD's healing power with scriptures, books on healing, and You Tube videos about healing, including those on her own channel. We talk, share and pray regularly, and she has been a blessing to me as GOD continues to answer my prayers. This morning, I opened one of my books entitled "GOD, Medicine Healing," by Daniel Fountain. The page that opened included the scripture **Genesis 1:26-27** which says, "GOD made us in HIS image. Dr. Fountain says "sin and disease can distort that image if it brings into our soul fear, anger, shame, depression or bitterness. (Remember, if you have accepted CHRIST, HIS Image will never leave your soul.) GOD wants to restore that image in the soul to help heal the body. My healing season has been a Blessing, because I am closer to GOD than I have ever been. May your healing season be just as Blessed.

Key Bible Verse

Genesis 1:26-27 – "Then God said, "Let us make mankind in our image, in our likeness, so that they may rule over the fish in the sea and the birds in the sky, over the livestock and all the wild animals, and over all the creatures that move along the ground." So God created mankind in his own image, in the image of God he created them; male and female he created them."

Prayers & Notes

_____

_____

_____

December 6

In a capitalist society like ours, we either work for a wage or sell a product to make a profit. Either way, the thought or hope is that we will get paid what we are worth. On the other hand, a gift is something given to us that we did not earn or necessarily deserve. The Apostle Paul used these terms to describe sin and death compared to the gift and grace of CHRIST in the **Romans 6**. He reminded those early Christians that sin produces a paycheck (wage), and you get what you deserve: death. **Romans 6:23** says, "the wages of sin is death." In this context, death means anything that is not from GOD, including fear, shame and physical death. On the other hand, Paul reminded those Christians that JESUS died for their sins, and that resulted in the gifts of Grace and Eternal Life. HE did the same thing for you and me. You see, the early Christians didn't deserve this gift of Grace and neither do Christians today. So thank HIM daily, will you?

Key Bible Verse

Romans 6:23 – "For the wages of sin is death, but the gift of God is eternal life in Christ Jesus our Lord."

Prayers & Notes

_____

_____

_____

_____

A Blessing from Yesterday _____

Something I am Thankful for Today _____

Patrick E. Moore

December 7

I have five, beautiful grandchildren who are polite, loving and each unique in their own special ways, and Karen and I love spending time with them. Recently, my 12-year-old grandson was with me in the car going or coming from some adventure we were having, and somehow the subject of GOD came up. He said, "Pops, I am a little confused about GOD being 3 people." I hope I answered it adequately. I was reminded of that conversation this morning when I read **John 14:26** which says, "but the helper, the Holy Spirit, whom the FATHER will send in MY Name; HE will teach you all things, that I said to you." In some translations, the word "Counselor" is used in lieu of "Helper." The HOLY SPIRIT is GOD, just the spirit version, like JESUS was the earthy version. We are living in uncertain times, and we need the HOLY SPIRIT to guide us toward Truth daily. HE will if we let HIM.

Key Bible Verse

John 14:26 – "But the Advocate, the Holy Spirit, whom the Father will send in my name, will teach you all things and will remind you of everything I have said to you."

Prayers & Notes

A Blessing from Yesterday _____

Something I am Thankful for Today _____

December 8

There is a game called "Who am I?," and it is ideal for groups of people who don't know each other very well. It helps break the ice by forcing you to ask "yes" or "no" questions in order to figure out what famous name is on the name tag stuck on the other person's back. Ever play it? It's an old game, but it came to mind yesterday while I listened to the song "Who am I?" sung by the Christian group Casting Crowns. The premise is how amazing it is to think THE CREATOR of Heaven and Earth knows who I am. He knows us regardless of who we are, our status in life, our past or future sins, our brokenness or even our devotion to HIM. The lyrics say it all, "it's not because of who I am or what I have done; it's because of what HE has done and who HE is." In **Ephesians 2:8-9**, Paul says, "For it by grace you have been saved through faith – and this is not from yourselves, it is the gift of GOD – not by works, so no one can boast." All Glory to HIS NAME.

Key Bible Verse

Ephesians 2:8-9 – "For it is by grace you have been saved, through faith – and this is not from yourselves, it is the gift of God – not by works, so that no one can boast."

Prayers & Notes

_____

_____

_____

A Blessing from Yesterday _____

Something I am Thankful for Today _____

Patrick E. Moore

December 9

Do you believe in miracles? Do you pray for them and expect them? We should, because **John 14:12-14** tells us, if we use GOD's WORDS in our prayers to the Heavenly FATHER, great things will occur to glorify JESUS. After all, don't we lift of petitions in prayers, and isn't there a request for a miracle in each petition? Remember, our prayers are powerful, so pray continuously because GOD's WORD will not be returned void **Isaiah 55:11**. We must hear GOD's WORD first, then our faith comes from speaking GOD's WORD, which includes our prayers. Try praying out loud. That is what I do each morning. There is nothing better for your Faith than hearing GOD's WORDS spoken from your own mouth.

✝

Key Bible Verse

Isaiah 55:11 – "so is my word that goes out from my mouth: It will not return to me empty but will accomplish what I desire and achieve the purpose for which I sent it."

Prayers & Notes

_____

_____

_____

_____

A Blessing from Yesterday _____

Something I am Thankful for Today _____

No Mountain Too High

December 10

This year has been a wild ride, huh? It's like an out-of-control carousel ride spinning faster and faster, horses bucking up and down like a bronco rodeo act, and all we can do it to hang on for dear life hoping it will stop. Sound about right? The "carosella" was developed by the French in the 1600's, but the original idea came from Europeans returning from the Crusades in the 1100's who had seen Turkish and Arabian horsemen participating in a game similar to jousting. The European soldiers built a wooden horse on planks in a wooden rink, and they would spin it around as the rider practiced jousting. Later, the French made a carnival ride. Yes, Christians, our world could be spinning out of control in the earthly realm, but we need to keep our hearts, minds and spirits grounded in the stable, spiritual realm. JESUS said in **John 14:27**, "Peace I leave with you; MY peace I give you. I do not give you as the world gives. Do not let your hearts be troubled and do not be afraid." Let GOD stop the dizziness today!

Key Bible Verse

John 14:27 – "Peace I leave with you; my peace I give you. I do not give to you as the world gives. Do not let your hearts be troubled and do not be afraid."

Prayers & Notes

_____

_____

_____

A Blessing from Yesterday _____

Something I am Thankful for Today _____

Patrick E. Moore

December 11

Let's talk about some positive news of the pandemic. Families are back together, eating together, loving on each other, praying together and, yes, turning to the LORD. GOD must like that, huh? Some think GOD's people are coming together in a revival of sorts. Even the Wall Street Journal wrote an article entitled "A Coronavirus Great Awakening." The article reminded us our country went through a spiritual revival for decades after the pain of WW2. During that time, 75% of our country went to a church or synagogue, prayers were allowed in school, and in 1954 we added "in GOD we trust" to our money. But it's been 75 years since the cataclysmic events of that war, and church attendance is down, prayer is gone from schools, addiction and suicides have increased, and over 40 million unwanted children are aborted each year around the world. Boy, does our country and world need a revival. Pray this virus is bringing GOD's people back together. **Isaiah 40:29-31** says, "but those who hope in the Lord will renew their strength. They will soar on wings like eagles; they will run and not grow weary; they will walk and not be faint." May GOD bless You today!

Key Bible Verse

Isaiah 40:31 – "but those who hope in the LORD will renew their strength. They will soar on wings like eagles; they will run and not grow weary; they will walk and not be faint."

Prayers & Notes

December 12

Do you typically use and trust the mirrors in your car to help you make turns and change lanes, or do you turn your head around to make sure your way is clear? I am totally a mirror guy. A few days ago, I shared an analogy of a rear-view mirror with a friend. I'm not sure how many years ago I thought of this, but my spiritual life was such that I would only see GOD in the "rear view mirror of my life." In other words, I looked at where GOD had been in my past; where HE had protected me, saved me, healed me or directed my life. I prayed at that time that I would begin seeing GOD out of the front windshield of my life and not just the rear-view mirror. GOD taught me that I probably could not handle knowing what was coming. Now, as my Faith has grown, I am excited to share that I see GOD out of the side windows of my life, all day long, in the things I see and the people I interact with. It's a great place to be. Today, thank GOD for where HE has been in your past and where HE is today. Trust GOD in where HE is leading you. "Blessed are the pure of heart, for they shall see GOD" (**Matthew 5:8**).

Key Bible Verse

Matthew 5:8. – "Blessed are the pure in heart, for they will see God."

Prayers & Notes

_____

_____

_____

_____

_____

Patrick E. Moore

December 13

Have you noticed like I have that there seem to be more Christmas lights up this year than last, and they were up earlier? My theory is that 2020 has been so dreary and dark that people wanted to share and enjoy the glowing colors of Christmas lights even more this year because they brighten up the world. Aren't you glad we don't live in a world without color? I love all the beautiful shades of color. You can thank GOD for creating light of different wavelengths that create colors. The first mention of a color in the Bible is in **Genesis 1:30** when it describes green herbs as part of creation, but the first prominent use of color occurs in **Genesis 9:13** when GOD puts a rainbow in the sky after the flood to remind us of HIS covenant with HIS people to never destroy the world by flood again. This Christmas, when you see all the beautiful shades of color, remember the beautiful shades of LOVE that GOD shares with those who know HIM. Let HIS Light shine in your life today!

Key Bible Verse

Genesis 1:30 – "And to all the beasts of the earth and all the birds in the sky and all the creatures that move along the ground—everything that has the breath of life in it—I give every green plant for food." And it was so."

Prayers & Notes

_____

_____

_____

_____

_____

December 14

An interesting event will occur on December 21ˢᵗ. Called the "Christmas Star" by some, it's a celestial event that hasn't been seen by humanity in over 800 years. The alignment of Jupiter and Saturn will appear as an incredible, bright star. Interestingly, it will appear on the day of Winter Solstice which is the shortest day of light and longest day of darkness during the year. Maybe this was what the Magi were following when they found the baby JESUS, the King of Kings. During that time, there was chaos, violence and division of people, similar to what we see in our world today. You know, the Creator of the heavens knew we needed a special reminder of HIS light this Christmas, so this event is no accident or coincidence. When you see a bright star in the sky, be reminded that JESUS came to bring light to a dark world for you and me. **John 12:46.**

✝

Key Bible Verse

John 12:46 – "I have come into the world as a light, so that no one who believes in me should stay in darkness."

Prayers & Notes

_____

_____

_____

_____

A Blessing from Yesterday _____

Something I am Thankful for Today _____

December 15

Did you know that we all have something in common...besides all having a cell phone? Yes, in fact we all have had this in the past, we all have it now, and we will all have it in the future while on this side of Heaven. What we have in common is pain. Yes, pain. It is because of the fall of man in the Garden of Eden. There are lots of different types of pain. We could have physical pain, emotional pain, and/or relational pain. Maybe your pain has to do with your Faith, because you think GOD is absent or silent in your time of need. However, if we keep our eyes on JESUS, HE will help us find purpose through our pain. **James 1:2-4** tells us we should consider it pure joy when we face trials because it leads to perseverance, which leads to the completion of our faith and therefore finding our purpose in HIM. Remember, JESUS relates to our pain because he felt all of it for <u>all</u> of mankind. Stay strong in your Faith today.

Key Bible Verse

James 1:2-4 – "Consider it pure joy, my brothers and sisters, whenever you face trials of many kinds, because you know that the testing of your faith produces perseverance. Let perseverance finish its work so that you may be mature and complete, not lacking anything."

Prayers & Notes

_____

_____

_____

A Blessing from Yesterday _____

Something I am Thankful for Today _____

December 16

Ok, let's do a rhetorical survey. From the physical perspective only, do you like the winter season better than the others? If you live in a winter wonderland location and you enjoy outdoor winter sports, it may be your favorite. Honestly, for me in Middle Tennessee, the cold, wet weather and dormant landscape makes winter my least favorite...with one exception: the thirty days of the Christmas season. I love the music, the mood, the lights and the celebration of the birth of CHRIST, our LORD and SAVIOR. This brings me to seasons in the spiritual realm, which come and go with seemingly no earthly reason. Those seasons can be difficult, sad or joyful, but know that GOD has a purpose for each one **Ecclesiastes 3:1** reminds us "There is a time for everything, and a season for every activity under the heavens." This year, during the Christmas season, remember GOD has a purpose for everything, and lean into your Faith, regardless of what season you are in.

✝

Key Bible Verse

Ecclesiastes 3:1 – "There is a time for everything, and a season for every activity under the heavens:"

Prayers & Notes

_____

_____

_____

A Blessing from Yesterday _____

Something I am Thankful for Today _____

Patrick E. Moore

December 17

A couple of mornings ago, I was walking through an enclosed outdoor area that had some bales of hay stacked up in the corner, and I am pretty sure I smelled the distinct smell of the bales before I saw them. You see, my twin brother and I tossed and stacked bales of hay on our grandparents' farm when we were teenagers, so I know the smell. But that morning, I didn't think of my youth; I thought about my Savior's birth in a manger. **Luke 2:7**. With no room in an inn, Mary, with child, and Joseph were given a stable normally used for the livestock. You can imagine the smell of hay surely filled the stable, and Mary probably used that hay to make a manger bed in which to lay her baby...JESUS. "Manger" comes from the Greek word "to eat," and it is no accident that a manger is an important symbol of this story, because JESUS, as the living word, is our Bread of Life. Partake of HIS WORD today!

Key Bible Verse

Luke 2:7 – "and she gave birth to her firstborn, a son. She wrapped him in cloths and placed him in a manger, because there was no guest room available for them."

Prayers & Notes

_____

_____

_____

A Blessing from Yesterday _____

Something I am Thankful for Today _____

December 18

Do you know what a sonnet is? It is a type of poem originating from an Italian poet in the 13th century. It comes from the Italian word "sonneto," which means "little poem." A sonnet has 14 lines/verses and a strict rhythmic scheme and structure. Elizabeth Barrett Browning, a devout Christian poet, wrote 44 sonnets in 1845-46. One of her most famous is Sonnet 43 which starts with the familiar verse, "How do I love thee, let me count the ways. I love thee to the depth, breadth and height." I am sure those lines sound familiar to you as well. Those words reminded me of how much GOD loves us and how he shows HIS love to us in so many ways. Real Love is not just a feeling, it is also caring, which causes actions. Read **Isaiah 54:10,** and you will find GOD's steadfast love will never leave us. Thank GOD today for HIS Love.

Key Bible Verse

Isaiah 54:10 – "Though the mountains be shaken, and the hills be removed, yet my unfailing love for you will not be shaken nor my covenant of peace be removed," says the LORD, who has compassion on you."

Prayers & Notes

_____

_____

_____

_____

A Blessing from Yesterday _____

Something I am Thankful for Today _____

Patrick E. Moore

December 19

We are now within one week of December 25th, the day we celebrate the birth of CHRIST. Can you believe it is almost Christmas? The Christian community hasn't always celebrated the birth of CHRIST on this day. It was changed by the Catholic Church to December 25th around 376 A.D., according to records of history. According to Biblical records and the account of shepherds in the field during the birth, the actual date was likely sometime in September. Why change it? The Church wanted to discourage the pagan celebration of Solstice marking the shortest day of the year so it was really a celebration of the sun (sol) overcoming darkness. It is fitting that the Christian Church wanted to replace that holiday with a celebration not of the sun, but of the one who *made* the sun. May this week become an intentional time to celebrate the birth of the one and only CHRIST, the one who came to die for our sins and bring us eternal life. **John 3:16.**

Key Bible Verse

John 3:16 – "For God so loved the world that he gave his one and only Son, that whoever believes in him shall not perish but have eternal life."

Prayers & Notes

_____

_____

_____

A Blessing from Yesterday _____

Something I am Thankful for Today _____

December 20

Yesterday, while driving home from some Christmas errands, I heard the popular song. "Angels We Have Heard on High." I sang along, as many of you would, too, and then wondered what the words "Gloria in Excelsis Deo" really mean and where they came from. First of all, these Latin words are translated as "Glory to GOD in the Highest." The song begins with the words the angels sang to the shepherds to announce the birth of CHRIST. These Latin lyrics began as a poem in the late 4th century and are now sung all over the world during the Christmas season. Just imagine the thrill and wonderment the shepherds must have felt when hearing the angels sing to announce the birth of the Great Shepherd. **Luke 2:13-14.** I look forward to hearing the angels sing one day, don't you? Remember to Praise GOD, when you hear that song this week.

✝

Key Bible Verse

Luke 2:13-14 – "Suddenly a great company of the heavenly host appeared with the angel, praising God and saying, "Glory to God in the highest heaven, and on earth peace to those on whom his favor rests."

Prayers & Notes

_____

_____

_____

A Blessing from Yesterday _____

Something I am Thankful for Today _____

Patrick E. Moore

December 21

Yesterday was gift wrapping day in the rec room, and since I have big, clumsy fingers, gift wrapping is really not my gift (pun intended). My wife asks me to wrap the oversized presents that need to be pieced together as well as my presents to her while she neatly wraps the kids' and grand-kids' presents. I am ok with that. Speaking of gifts, studies show 60% of Americans buy their presents the week of Christmas, and then 1.5 million of those presents are returned on Jan. 3rd. We know someone who gives perfect gifts: our Heavenly FATHER. Yes, HE gives each of us perfect gifts that never have to be returned, gifts to help one another know CHRIST better. His gifts described in **1 Corinthians 12:9-11** include wisdom, healing, prophesizing, speaking in tongues, discernment and others. Our job to remove HIS Gifts from under our internal spiritual tree and unwrap them and use those gifts to the fullest. Thank HIM today for your gifts.

Key Bible Verse

1 Corinthians 12:11 – "All these are the work of one and the same Spirit, and he distributes them to each one, just as he determines."

Prayers & Notes

_____

_____

_____

A Blessing from Yesterday _____

Something I am Thankful for Today _____

December 22

Remember this children's poem? "Star light, star bright, first star I see tonight, I wish I may, I wish I might, have the wish I wish tonight!" Well, that poem came to mind last night as Karen and I gazed at the bright star in the sky some call the Christmas Star of 2020. A rare alignment of Saturn and Jupiter made them look like one bright star, even though their orbits are over 200 million miles apart. The entire world had the opportunity to see this rare event for the first time in over 800 years. Last night also reminded me of how awesome our GOD is because HE created the Heavens and the Earth. **Genesis1:1.** My wish last night was that we, as Christians, share the awesome nature of GOD with others so they can also have Peace on Earth. Praise HIM!

✝

Key Bible Verse

Genesis 1:1 – "In the beginning God created the heavens and the earth."

Prayers & Notes

_____

_____

_____

_____

_____

A Blessing from Yesterday _____

Something I am Thankful for Today _____

Patrick E. Moore

December 23

One of the most popular Christian carols you will hear during Christmas is "Angels We Have Heard on High," and it certainly is one of my favorites. I have been singing along all week whenever I hear it. You can search the web and see arrangements of this song sung by everyone from country, pop and Christian artists to Andrea a Bocelli, the great opera singer. Even though this carol, originally written in Latin, was attributed to Saint Hilary of Poitiers in the mid 4th century, the idea for the song goes back to JESUS' birth when a multitude of heavenly hosts sang "Glory to GOD on the Highest" to announce to the shepherds the birth of CHRIST in the city of David. The account can be found in **Luke 2:13-14** I am going to play that song as I read the CHRISTmas story in **Luke 2:1-20** to my family during our gathering on Christmas Eve. Remember these verses and this song as we celebrate the birth of JESUS this Christmas Day.

Key Bible Verse

Luke 2:13-14 – "Suddenly a great company of the heavenly host appeared with the angel, praising God and saying, "Glory to God in the highest heaven, and on earth peace to those on whom his favor rests.""

Prayers & Notes

_____

_____

_____

A Blessing from Yesterday _____

Something I am Thankful for Today _____

December 24

Today is Christmas Eve, a usually a joyous occasion in anticipation of Christmas morning. You may not know that it even stopped the fighting in WW1 for a few days. It was 1914 in the muddy trenches of Europe when American and German troops had a truce on Christmas Eve. Both countries came from a Christian background, and that night you could hear "Silent Night" being sung from both sides. Trenches were decorated with paper lanterns, some of the troops met between the lines to exchange gifts (usually tobacco, chocolate or food rations), and it was labeled the Christmas Truce of 2014. It was never reported to happen again. Christmas Eve is a special time for our family because we gather at our house to celebrate Christmas. This year, we are adding our own church service along with the observance of the LORD's Supper. May you have a Blessed Christmas Eve in anticipation of JESUS' birthday tomorrow. **Isaiah 7:14**.

Key Bible Verse

Isaiah 7:14 – "Therefore the Lord himself will give you a sign: The virgin will conceive and give birth to a son and will call him Immanuel."

Prayers & Notes

_____

_____

_____

A Blessing from Yesterday _____

Something I am Thankful for Today _____

Patrick E. Moore

December 25

Happy Birthday, JESUS. The highlight of our family Christmas celebration last night was letting the grandkids lead in worship before dinner and the gift exchange. The kids read the Christmas story account from **Luke 2**, conducted a perfect communion (whew, no grape juice spills on the white carpet), and we closed with singing Silent Night by candlelight (birthday candles, no less). It was a perfect night. Speaking of JESUS' birth, read **Isaiah 9:6** and realize that the prophet Isaiah was prophesizing the birth of JESUS 700 years in advance. Why? Because the Jewish people were going to be defeated, captured and exiled by the Assyrians and would need hope during dark times that a KING would be coming. Today, a lot of people are experiencing dark times, but fear not and have Faith. The KING, yes, JESUS, is coming back. Merry Christmas!

✝

Key Bible Verse

Isaiah 9:6 – "or to us a child is born, to us a son is given, and the government will be on his shoulders. And he will be called Wonderful Counselor, Mighty God, Everlasting Father, Prince of Peace."

Prayers & Notes

_____

_____

_____

_____

A Blessing from Yesterday _____

Something I am Thankful for Today _____

December 26

I hope everyone had as wonderful a Christmas as we did. When we called our 9-year-old granddaughter to see what Santa brought her, she gleefully stated, "Can you believe it? We have our first white Christmas!", which was really funny because we got a slight dusting of snow that couldn't have been measured on a ruler. But, it gave her a good feeling and memory. I then wondered if JESUS ever saw snow, so I started researching with Google. I couldn't confirm it, but we could assume he saw it in the mountains in Israel where it is prevalent in December and January. Did you know that snow is mentioned twenty-three times in the Bible, and it always has a neutral or positive meaning? Several times, snow is used as a symbol for purity, such as with the angels' clothes mentioned in **Matthew 28:3,** or forgiveness as seen in **Psalms 51:7**. So, whether you have a foot of snow or just a dusting, let it remind you of the purity of JESUS and his gift of forgiveness.

✝

Key Bible Verse

Matthew 28:3 – "His appearance was like lightning, and his clothes were white as snow."

Prayers & Notes

_____

_____

_____

A Blessing from Yesterday _____

Something I am Thankful for Today _____

Patrick E. Moore

December 27

Yesterday, Karen asked me to transfer the Christmas photos from my phone to hers. I saw how many I had and realized I had to cull a few first. I had over sixty. Most of them were of the kids and grandkids, as they should be, and I began thanking GOD for allowing me to be a father and grandfather. It's my greatest accomplishment, besides marrying my wonderful wife who made all of it possible. But I am not perfect, and neither are you. We all have flaws, but, as Christians, we all have the perfect Father. Yes, our Heavenly FATHER. In addition, HE is our Everlasting FATHER and will never depart from us. That provides great comfort, right? In **Matthew 6:31-33**, JESUS tells the believers then, and instructs us now, not to worry about what we will eat, drink or the clothes we will wear because our Heavenly FATHER will provide everything we need. Do you know the Everlasting FATHER? Let's Praise HIM today!

Key Bible Verse

Matthew 6:31-33 – "So do not worry, saying, 'What shall we eat?' or 'What shall we drink?' or 'What shall we wear?' For the pagans run after all these things, and your heavenly Father knows that you need them. But seek first his kingdom and his righteousness, and all these things will be given to you as well."

Prayers & Notes

December 28

Have you ever wondered who pays for free shipping for online shipping? You do know it's not free, someone has to pay it. Let's take Amazon, for example. Their total shipping cost in 2019 was over 30 billion dollars. Wow. Who paid it? We did, either through increased price of the goods or through our Prime memberships. That brings me to the sermon I heard yesterday on JESUS paying our sin debt with HIS blood on the cross. We all have sinned and fallen short of the Glory of GOD. Someone had to pay that debt before we could have eternal life. This famous anonymous quote says it all, "JESUS paid a debt HE did not owe, and we owed a debt we could not pay." Thank GOD today for paying our sin debt...past, present and future.**1 John 2:2**. Remember that every time you see "free shipping."

Key Bible Verse

I John 2:2 – "He is the atoning sacrifice for our sins, and not only for ours but also for the sins of the whole world."

Prayers & Notes

_____

_____

_____

_____

A Blessing from Yesterday _____

Something I am Thankful for Today _____

Patrick E. Moore

December 29

Often times when we discuss or study the Bible, we consider what the culture was doing or thinking at the time of its writing, to try to put things into context. What is culture? "Culture" derives from the Latin word "colere" which means "to tend to the earth, grow, cultivate, and nurture." Culture affects language, music, religion, cuisine, social habits and the arts. If you read **Genesis 3:8**, you will find the culture of Adam and Eve prior to the fall was pretty perfect. What happened? Simply stated, the culture went from pleasing GOD to pleasing man. Remember these two important things. Our culture is ever changing and slipping further and further away from GOD and has no redeeming eternal consequence. Even though culture may change, GOD's Commands don't. We are commanded to love GOD and to obey HIS commands. **1 John 5:3**. Don't let your culture take your eyes off GOD. PRAISE HIM today!

✝

Key Bible Verse

1 John 5:3 – "In fact, this is love for God: to keep his commands. And his commands are not burdensome,"

Prayers & Notes

_____

_____

_____

A Blessing from Yesterday _____

Something I am Thankful for Today _____

December 30

Be honest, do you know the difference between "orthodoxy" and "orthopraxy" as it pertains to our Faith? I didn't until recently when I heard the latter ("orthopraxy") in an office Bible study. Frankly, I didn't know how to spell it, and evidently Facebook doesn't either because it underlines the word as if it is spelled wrong. Orthodoxy is the general, and accepted, doctrine and theology of our Faith. Orthopraxy is the correct conduct, both ethically and Biblically. Which comes first? Orthodoxy comes first, because if we understand the doctrine of our Christian Faith first, primarily from the teachings of JESUS, then we should know how to live our lives in JESUS-like conduct. **James 2:14** says, "What good is it, my brothers and sisters, if someone claims to have faith but has no deeds? Can such faith save them?" Let's strive for both each day.

Key Bible Verse

James 2:14 –"What good is it, my brothers and sisters, if someone claims to have faith but has no deeds? Can such faith save them?"

Prayers & Notes

_____

_____

_____

_____

A Blessing from Yesterday _____

Something I am Thankful for Today _____

Patrick E. Moore

December 31

Today is New Year's Eve, signifying the closing of one year and the dawning of a new one. From the physical realm perspective, this has been a difficult year for all of us, but from the spiritual realm standpoint, it has been my greatest. What do I mean? Our physical body resides in the physical realm, which Satan controls, and he has tried to wreak havoc with a pandemic. Our Faith, as Christians, resides in the Spiritual realm controlled by the FATHER, the SON and the HOLY SPIRIT. Because of GOD's WORD and HIS Grace, my Faith has grown during this year. Remember, GOD has a plan already mapped out for us in 2021. **Isaiah 43:18-19** says, ""Forget the former things; do not dwell on the past. See, I am doing a new thing! Now it springs up; do you not perceive it? I am making a way in the wilderness and streams in the wasteland." Are you ready for great things in 2021? I am. In order to receive the blessing GOD has in store for us, we must read and meditate on HIS WORD daily then speak that Good News to those we come in contact with. Get ready for a great new year. Happy New Year!

✝

Key Bible Verse

Isaiah 43:18-19 - "Forget the former things; do not dwell on the past. See, I am doing a new thing! Now it springs up; do you not perceive it? I am making a way in the wilderness and streams in the wasteland."

Prayers & Notes

Pat's Family

Pat & Karen

Daughter-Michele, Karen & Daughter-Julie

Sister-in-law Corinne, Twin Brother Moose

Moose, Carole, Jayne & Pat, the Siblings

Back Row - Mallory, Karen, Pat, Jackson & Bo

Front Row – Maddox & Mason

The Family at Auburn

Patrick E. Moore

What Others Have Said, Part 2

Studying God's word and focusing on His plan for my life has kept me from spinning off my base. I thoroughly enjoy Pat Moore's daily healing thoughts. There have been many good events, but many disasters. Reading Pat's daily thoughts has helped me realize and acknowledge Who is in charge. "Praise God from Whom all blessings flow. Praise him all creatures here below. Praise Him above ye heavenly hosts. Praise Father, Son, and Holy Ghost!" *Susan Coles*

Pat, your daily reflections are heartfelt and Spirit led. I appreciate your personal insight into where the Spirit is leading you as you apply God's word to your life. *Brad Thomason, Real Estate Developer.*

This year has tested the definition of community and extended its scope. I am very grateful to start my day with a Healing Thought that is centered in the Word. My mind is always blown by how God can speak to all of us and yet reach me as if I were the only one in the room. The Daily Healing Thoughts have been a great examples and good reminder of what others are going through, too. *Casia Phillips*

I certainly feel honored to be on your daily healing thoughts. I enjoy them very much. I realize how much thought and effort it requires to do this daily. Being able to take daily sights, thoughts and experiences and relate them to God's word as Biblically written is a true gift. GOD can do all things including healing. I share your message with our Bible study group here in East Tennessee. I need this daily spiritual boost some days more than others. We are related by family. You could be my brother, you are certainly my friend, and we are bonded together by Jesus Christ. Keep them coming. Stay healthy and safe. *Gene Simpson, Father-in-Law*

Pat's Daily Healing Thoughts have been a true blessing in my life! Each daily devotional includes a wonderful reminder of God's truth through a very personal real-life scenario, delivered in a very relevant and useful way. I look forward to reading this book in its entirety soon and for years to come!

Tina M Sasso, Nurse Practitioner

Every day I read your daily healing thought, I am reminded of the phrase, "The mind speaks to the body. Sometimes it is a fatal conversation." Your daily thoughts remind me to slow down, take stock and engage the mind as a powerful part of my wellness. You are a special blessing. *Frank P McGoff*

Pat's Daily Healing Thought comes to me each day via a text message. It usually arrives around 9 AM, and it is a wonderful way to start the day. It is always uplifting and meaningful. I love the fact that it draws in everyday life moments to highlight the fact that GOD is always present. It's a blessing to have Pat in my life. We have been friends for more than 25 year. Love you. *Jennifer Borislow,* Principal, Borislow Insurance

Pat has been a dear friend and spiritual mentor to me for 11 years. He is the reason I have found my walk with God. Pat is inspiring each of us with his love of the Word and God. He has a way of combining a prompting, or thought from his life experiences, while weaving in a small lesson in history or life, and then he ties in the perfect verse. It is a divinely fulfilling way to start the day. *Lisa Allain*

Pat's daily healing thoughts are a daily reminder of what Jesus did for me on the cross. We are to take up our cross daily and reflecting on the cross of Christ helps me to take up my own cross and fully surrender. His healing flows into my life in so many different ways, and I am always encouraged by how Jesus has worked in the life of others. Thank you for your daily encouragement, Pat!

Al Schierbaum

Patrick E. Moore

Pat, it has been such a blessing to receive, read, and meditate on your daily Biblical reflections and healing messages over this past year. For me, it has been like getting what some would call a "God wink" each day. You dared me to look at scripture with practical reflections of day-to-day life as a backdrop. This gave me a different view of my personal healing journey. For this I praise God and thank you. Blessings. *Susan Sawyer*

Your daily text is an additional reminder for me to "be still and know that the Lord is God." To stop and say, "thank you." To further realize the importance of God's word. All of our devotions and other "religious" books should be in addition and secondary to the Bible. Thank you for impressing that importance. God's Word is infallible, inerrant, and eternal. *Fred Shanks, Optometrist*

Pat is a great storyteller connects real life events/topics to the "soul" of individuals. He has a way of drawing all ages in and making things that could be difficult to understand very easy to put into place in our daily lives. I have found his daily treasures very helpful in putting me in a positive healing space and making my day much brighter which in turns help me be more positive with those I interact with! *Tammy Ralls, RN*

These devotions have been an inspiration with real life narratives of purpose and influence. They have helped me grow spiritually, gain a deeper understanding of the Bible and its teachings, and shown me how to apply the teachings in my life.

Anita Marshall, RN

I have known Pat Moore for 13 years and the Lord has used him in many ways in my life. To see his pursuit of Christ, and his desire to reflect his Lord and Savior is a testament to the Lord working in his life. Thankful to call him friend and brother. *Solomon Kafoure, Partner*

Very thankful for the "Daily Healing" emails that I receive every morning. During my quiet time, it is always encouraging to receive additional scripture that pertains to our everyday life. At times in life, it can feel that you are fighting a battle all alone through the peaks and valleys, but it is powerful to be reminded that we have God's love, grace, and mercy to get through it. By opening the daily healing message, I know that we are surrounded by believers who acknowledge we are broken in our sinful nature, but because of God's grace and mercy we can ask for forgiveness and focus on Him and his love each day and know that we can be saved. Thanks for sharing every morning! *Billy Haley, Financial Representative*

Pat's daily healing thoughts have been a catalyst for me to continue to thank God for all the blessings he has bestowed upon my family. They are also a reminder of God's ultimate power in healing and his infinite capacity for grace and love.

Neil Anderson, Retired Business Executive, High School friend and teammate.

I look forward every day to receiving The Daily Healing Thoughts. To me they are nourishment. I read them, chew them, then absorb them into my Spirit. Like breakfast energizes my body, they allow the battlefield of my mind to be alert. I am more prepared for the temptations of Satan and ready for the plan God has for me that day. I'm very thankful for your sharing, Pat. Sincerely, *Frank Dial*

Pat-I can't tell you how happy I was that just a little over a year ago, Peter and I spent time with you in Nashville and you told us about your DHT. Even though we are of different religious persuasions, both religions started with the same book. Based on your daily thoughts, more recent work has developed a special sense of peace and comfort which is especially relevant for today's trying times. Your book will work wonders for anyone with an open mind, of any religious persuasion. You have a special gift as a messenger of good. Blessings, *Mike Weintraub*

Patrick and I have been friendly for a long time initially seeded in industry activities. We would see each other annually and visit but our personal interaction had been limited. There was a meeting in his hometown in

October 2019 and I had reached out to see if he wanted to have lunch and also with another friend of ours. We did. Patrick picked us up at the hotel and interestingly enough took a risk to share with both of us about his significant commitment to Jesus, reading Scripture and centering his life in a profound link with God. He went on to say that he had formed the habit of texting "My Daily Healing Thought" as a way for him to be grounded each day and in turn share those thoughts with many others. Patrick's healing had initially been focused on a physical affliction, but has he prayed and studied more, his healing was on many levels. As a result, I asked him if he would include me on his daily texting list and believe I have received a text each and every day since. What Patrick feels and then shares with his friends, in Jesus' name, is quite compelling. It provides me with a daily anchor to read, think and consider the power of possibilities all emanating from God. It has given me countless opportunities to think, reflect and give thanks for the blessings in my life ... and in turn to be more aware and profoundly grateful. I say this with deep appreciation for the daily gift given selflessly from Patrick as he is acting as Jesus' instrument to spread his word. Amen. *Peter Sullivan*

I have suffered from Post-Traumatic Stress for 49 yrs. I have been through years and years of therapy, but the mind still tricks you into depression, hypervigilance, not sleeping 2 to 3 hrs. a night and questioning God's love. Pat's daily messages are truly healing and not just to the human mind but the Soul. To me it was a miracle meeting Pat and Karen. With all the hate, evil and un-Godly people in the world, Pat's daily words has been a Godsend to my hurting soul and I truly believe my Guardian Angel Peter (which I have met) put Pat and I together to bless me on earth. I can't wait to read Pats messages. *John Siverling, Vietnam Vet*

A true gift of taking scripture and applying it to current situations and events. Very well thought out and explained in down to earth terms. *Keith Gardner, CPA*

The Daily Thought broadens my spiritual thinking and sends me down a different path each morning that left on my own I would not find. *Al Carman, Businessman*

It is so beautiful how Pat takes an everyday occurrence or object and weaves it into a spiritual devotional that lifts our eyes and hearts toward Jesus. His words of encouragement help us find a deeper meaning in our everyday walk. *Christy Speer*

Your Daily Healing Thoughts are very positive thoughts that creates a thought inside that gives me the strength I need each day to maintain my sincere focus on the Almighty Jesus Christ. *Sayonara Howard, Shift Manager for Brueggers Bagels*

Pat Moore and I have been friends for over 35 years. We originally met when Pat was involved with our business planning. These were the years when I was interested in adding years to my life. Fast forward to the present time where my focus in adding life to my years. Thru my relationship with God, and with encouragement from Pat and his Daily Healing Thoughts, I am making progress.

Thank you Brother, and may God continue to bless you. *Wilson Doyle, Retired Businessman*

These daily healing thoughts bring my life back to a centered and grounded existence. I am reminded each day our LORD is in control. My humbleness and praise to GOD is the most important piece I give to each new day. Through these daily healing thoughts and keeping a heavenly perspective makes whatever each day brings to my life, a feeling of peace and comfort that GOD is in control. *Nicole Burgess*

The Daily Healing Thoughts that you send by email brings the Word to our attention. You do not know when it will provide the comfort and healing that is needed. Delivering that continuous flow feeds the heart and mind daily. For some, that may be the only daily feeding they get. It is a blessing. *Barb Westad*

My Daily Healing Thoughts have been my "manna" in the morning. Pat Moore has definitely changed the playing field concerning daily devotionals. The insights and scriptures are relevant and impactful. A recommended read! *Bishop Sandy McClain*

Suggested Reading

1. *A Small Book of Prayers for Great Big Power* – by Erica Diggs 2020

2. *Power of Healing* – John Wimber & Kevin Springer 1987

3. *The Healing Codes: Underlying Principles* – Dr. Jerry Graham 2013

4. *The Red Sea Rules:* The Same God Who Led You in Will Lead You Out – Robert J. Morgan 2014

5. *Goliath Must Fall*: Winning the Battle Against Your Giants – Louie Giglio 2017

6. *Surprised by the Power of the Spirit* – Discovering How God Speaks and Heals Today – Jack Deere 2020

7. *God, Medicine, and Miracles*: The Spiritual Factor in Healing – Daniel Fountain 2000

8. *The Purpose Driven Life*: What on Earth Am I Here For? – Rick Warren 2013

9. *The Prayer of Jabez* – Bruce Wilkinson & David Kopp 2005

10. *Balcony People*: From the Heart – Joyce Landorf Heatherly 1984

Patrick E. Moore

Made in the USA
Columbia, SC
06 May 2021